THE
SINGING
TEACHER

Wyatt House books may be ordered through booksellers or by contacting:

WYATT HOUSE PUBLISHING
399 Lakeview Dr. W.
Mobile, Alabama 36695
www.wyattpublishing.com
editor@wyattpublishing.com

Because of the dynamic nature of the Internet, any web address or links contained in this book may have changed since publication and may no longer be valid.

Cover and interior design by: Mark Wyatt

ISBN 13: 978-1-7326049-1-9

Printed in the United States of America

THE SINGING TEACHER

HOW THE WORSHIP LEADER SHAPES THE THEOLOGY OF THE CHURCH

ZEB BALENTINE

Wyatt House Publishing

Mobile, Alabama

The Singing Teacher is filled with strong biblical insights on worship, music, and lots of practical ideas for those who help others worship each week. This would be perfect for teams to read together, then discuss and debate some of the perspectives that Zeb Balentine brings up. A positive contribution to the Church's ongoing conversation about how and why we worship the way we do.

-Paul Baloche, Christian song-writer

Have you ever stumbled upon a restaurant that once tried, became a favorite place to eat for years to come? That's what "The Singing Teacher" is destined to become for all students of worship who find it. In this book, Zeb Balentine takes us inside the science, history, theology, and qualities of singing that cause it to be one of the most important discipleship tools the Church has in our hands. The next time someone asks you, "Why should it matter if people sing in church?", you will find yourself reaching to this book for the answer. I wish I had read it years ago.

-Mike Harland, Director of LifeWay Worship

The act of worship is an ability that God has given all of his creation. However, God knew we would struggle with this, see the First Commandment. Zeb addresses this issue by giving sound doctrinal advice on how leaders of worship are to guide, instruct, and teach through song. He also points out that God should be the focus of worship and not the leader. In an age of 'likes' and 'follows,' this book could not be more timely.

*-Jonathan Wilson, COO of
Kyser Musical Products*

As a Christian recording artist I appreciate Zeb's fresh perspective on teaching through singing. *The Singing Teacher* challenges every artist in the faith to sing and make music with purpose; to admonish God's people through the unique and extremely influential medium of song. This book is a must-read for the Christian artist, songwriter, and worship leader who has a desire to encourage and inspire others by teaching through singing.

-Dr. Lindsey Graham, Christian recording artist

The landscape of church culture has shifted over the last three decades. In many regards, we are witnessing a dumbing down of the church theologically and ultimately, spiritually. This era is there has also been a waning in the pursuit of Christian Education. Consequently, the Senior Pastor and Worship leader share an even greater responsibility in providing Spiritual Formation for the congregation in worship. As a result, it is important that there be a marriage between preaching and music. This book is a much needed tool for the worship leader and the Senior Pastor, as together they navigate the tempestuous waters of worship planning. Dr. Zeb Balentine has prayerfully written a book that will help Pastors and Worship Leaders plan and present the worship of God's people in spirit and in truth.

*-Dr. Eddie A. Robinson, Worship minister,
Springfield Baptist Church, Conyers, GA*

The Singing Teacher is full of sobering, gospel-centered truths about worship that every worship leader should take into consideration before stepping back on the stage.

> **-Will Price,** *Executive Pastor of Ministries,*
> *Calvary Chapel, Port Saint Lucy, FL*

This book is a must read for those who seek to know more about the profound gift that music has played and continues to play in the development of our theology as believers. It is an insightful look into the care we all must take in church leadership and in our family roles for ensuring our music is building the faith and leading people to a sound understanding of who God is.

> **-Rebekah Jones**, *Kids Choir and*
> *Music Academy Director, Saddleback Church*

Zeb Balentine offers great practical advice to leading worship as well as bringing insightful truths to the oldest form of expression. "The Singing Teacher" is filled with helpful hints and gentle reminders for worship leaders everywhere that we teach through song. His discernment into intermingling the two, music and Word, will be beneficial for years to come.

> **-Robb McCormick**, *Worship Pastor*
> *Fellowship of Christians Singer-Songwriter*

PREFACE

Little did I know, the summer before my junior year of high school that God was going to wreck my world. It was at summer church camp that I came to a clear realization that God was calling me into the ministry. He had been drawing me to this for quite some time, but I found myself subconsciously rebelling against it. In my mind, if I sinned enough God would forget about this whole ministry thing, and move on, and call someone else instead. But, that's not how God works. He loves to take broken people and restore them. God proves His might by taking those you least expect and call them to fulfill His purpose.

When news began to spread about my decision to embrace God's call, everyone assumed I would be going into music ministry. I quickly passed on that idea, at least for the time being. See, I was a metal-head, rock-star wannabe. I had posters of bands and rock musicians covering every inch of my bedroom walls. I wore my hair long and played my music loud. The idea of devoting my life to singing songs in a suit and tie, in a setting where if you had drums and electric guitars, they better be turned down low enough that you couldn't hear them did NOT appeal to me in the least.

What I did have was a desire to teach the Bible. I began to teach at any opportunity that I was given. God opened up for me some really incredible opportunities for me to teach and preach that I didn't appreciate fully until later in life. I didn't attend Bible college to earn a degree in church music or worship arts, but to train as a preaching pastor. When I wasn't socializing, I eventually obtained a degree in Biblical Studies with an emphasis on Pastoral Ministry. I had no idea at the time that this approach to my education would one day shape my philosophy and approach to leading worship.

Meanwhile, music ministry was something I did, not because I felt called, but because I was a guy with a guitar that could sing. I began to discover that I was having more opportunities to lead worship rather than to preach. This frustrated me, but I rolled with it. For some time I still resisted music ministry because I preferred to teach rather than sing. I entered vocational ministry in 2006 as a youth and music minister. I was a youth minister because I loved to disciple students through God's Word, and I also served in music ministry so I could find work, because I wasn't talented enough in either field at the time. That's not to say people serving in dual roles aren't talented to do one or the other, but in my case I was not.

God helped me realize that to follow the call into music ministry was not to say "goodbye" to a teaching ministry, but that music ministry IS a teaching ministry. I began to understand the significant role a worship leader has in shaping the doctrinal beliefs of the people he leads. I studied what the Scriptures had to say on the matter, and I discovered the Bible is filled with examples of songs shaping the beliefs of the worshiper. This revelation ignited a renewed focus on my life's calling. God clarified for me that he had given me musical abilities and a passion for the Bible and theology and it was His design for those things to be used as effective tools to make disciples.

This book is a representation of what God has shown me, and is continuing to show me through His Word about how worship leaders play a significant role in shaping the theology of the church.

CHAPTER 1

SINGING AND SCRIPTURE MEMORY

*"Let the word of Christ **dwell in you richly**, teaching and admonishing one another in all wisdom, singing psalms and hymns and spiritual songs, with thankfulness in your hearts to God."*

- Colossians 3:16

When I was in Bible College I studied Greek for two years (If you are impressed by that just keep reading). I am no Greek scholar by any stretch of the imagination. The first year was difficult because it consisted of learning a ton of vocabulary words, and even worse, all of the grammar rules for the language. But the second year was when we learned to put that information to practical use...at least that was the design. The exams for this class required us to translate entire chapters of the New Testament from

Greek to English. This sounds like fun—and it was—for a good Greek student. While most of my classmates were in their dorms or apartments the night before brushing up on their vocabulary words and grammar, I was writing songs. I discovered I could invent melodies and find a way to turn entire chapters of Scripture (in the English translation) into songs so I could commit the passage to memory more quickly and could recall it more easily. The next day during the test, I would quietly sing the song and write down the English translation of the Greek text.

Now, some might call this method "cheating," but I would say…okay, maybe it was cheating. Hey, Greek student that might be reading this, whatever you do, don't follow my example. God will smite you. I'm just trying to prove a point here. Anyway, I learned a ton of Scripture that year, and I also learned a valuable lesson: SINGING the Word of God helps us REMEMBER the Word of God.

I don't know why it took me so long to realize this. Learning through singing has been an educational method for years. Think about this: How did you learn your ABCs? Did you sit in your kindergarten class memorizing alphabet flash cards? Did you sit through a power-point presentation, or did the teacher give hour-long lectures on the alphabet? Probably not. Most of us were taught the alphabet by learning the song. There's a good reason for this. Melodies have a unique way of sticking in our minds for a long time. Why is that? Perhaps God has designed it to be this way. This is a huge reason why we sing together in our church gatherings. Who knows all of the intentions God had when He designed us to be prone to remember melodies and song lyrics, but one of the most significant and clearest reasons we see in Scripture is so we can learn, memorize, and take to heart great truths about who He is and what He has done.

Colossians 3:16 is one of those verses that changed my perspective on music ministry and helped me see how important it is. The indwelling word, the teaching, and the admonishing is not a separate idea from the call to sing "psalms and hymns and spiritual songs." For the intention of this verse to be properly understood, try reading it like this: "Let the word of Christ dwell in you richly, teaching and admonishing one another in all wisdom, [BY] singing psalms and hymns and spiritual songs…" You can see the purpose of this verse a little clearer now, can't you? If you want to learn or memorize something…SING IT.

Bob Kauflin put it this way, "Our brains are hard wired to recognize, categorize, and remember patterns in music better than we remember those patterns when we are just talking."[1] He adds, "Music helps us remember words—and God intends for music to help us remember the word of Christ."[2]

Singing Scripture causes it to dwell within us, and to dwell within us RICHLY. Singing commits Scripture to memory in ways other memorization methods fall short of doing.

AN AUDIENCE OF ONE?

You've probably heard it said (or even said it yourself) that when we worship or are leading in worship we are singing to "an audience of One." It has become one of those worship clichés that

---

1   Bob Kauflin, *Why do we Sing?*
2   Bob Kauflin, *Worship Matters*, 104.

are said frequently, but isn't entirely biblical.[3]

I understand the intention behind the phrase, which is to move away from a performance mentality of worship or worship-leading and to focus on God alone. As people who help to lead the church in worship, it is important we are on constant guard against the rock-star mentality. No matter our original intent for being on a platform, our flesh can take that and create within us a deep craving to be praised and adored.

The problem with this saying, however, is it can also take away from a very clear intention that God had in mind for congregational singing. Our worship gatherings are not only meant to be vertical (to God), but they are also meant to be horizontal. Is this man-centered worship? Not at all. But, I do believe Scripture and logic teaches even though worship is Christ-centered and God is the only object of our worship, the worshipers will be edified as they participate. This is God's design. God commands us to sing not exclusively to Him, but to and with each other. Notice the phrase "one another" in Colossians 3:16. We are also told in Ephesians 5:19 to address "ONE ANOTHER in psalms and hymns and spiritual songs."

If you want to sing like it's just you and God in the room, this is what our private times of worship are supposed to look like. After all, Sunday mornings in church buildings are not the only time and place that we can or should worship. But when the church is gathered to worship together, we are told that we sing truth to each other. But why? What is this accomplishing? When we sing the Word of God together, it is dwelling within us. We are learning it,

---

3   Much like Matthew 18:20 being wrongly applied to small worship gatherings, when the verse is actually in the context of church discipline.

committing it to memory, filling our souls with it.

I would argue that music impacts our memories when it is a communal act, rather than simply a private one. There have been numerous times I've listened to or played music while alone, but those times have been mostly forgotten. But I can remember every single concert that I've ever been to like they happened yesterday. I recall my High School years, driving up and down the roads with my friend Chris, and blasting Bon Jovi through the speakers. To this day, I can still sing all of the lyrics. I think part of the reason for this is because when many others are in the same room, singing the same song to and with one another, our brains are designed to take notice. Our minds realize there is a significant event going on. Therefore, our brains store these memories in a good place that won't be easily forgotten.

Now, granted, I don't remember every single worship service I've ever been in, but I can tell you that times of singing in corporate worship have stuck in my memories more than singing moments of private worship. I don't apologize for that, because I believe that is how God has made our brains to function. God desires for us to sing not only to Him, but to one another. Singing Scripture songs with fellow believers as the gathered church will help to imbed God's Word into our hearts and minds, causing it to dwell in us richly.

WHAT IS LEARNED IN SONG IS REMEMBERED LONG

Someone told me about a ministry event they attended which featured Pam Tebow (the mother of Christian athlete, Tim Tebow) as the guest speaker. My acquaintance rehashed some things that

Pam had said and to be honest, I was only halfway paying attention because I am not really the biggest sports fan in the world. I have as much athletic ability as Bill Gates.

Needless to say, I wasn't on the edge of my seat wanting to hear what Mrs. Tebow had to say. But then my friend proceeded to talk about things Pam did when raising her children. Because I was a new dad, this caused to me to pay closer attention. I was told that Pam used to make up little songs with Scripture as the lyrics and she sang them to her kids. That was nothing new to me. I have heard of that before (remember my Greek class?). But my friend quoted Pam as saying, "What is learned in song is remembered long." That grabbed my attention and I thought: "That…is…BRIL-LIANT." Since then I have applied that philosophy to my music ministry and the importance of worship leaders and their responsibility to lead their congregations to sing the words of Scripture.

This obviously isn't a new concept. That little phrase may not have even been original to Mrs. Tebow. But, God's worshipers have been singing Scripture songs for several millennia. Old Testament saints sang the Psalms which were divinely inspired Scripture. Psalm 119 is the longest Psalm and is a worship song specifically about God's Word. It's not an accident that the longest song in the Hebrew Hymnal was about the Scriptures and how they should remain within us. The early church also sang the Psalms as well as New Testament passages set to music. Thanks to modern-day worship leaders and songwriters, we can't hardly read the Psalms or the New Testament Epistles without coming across a verse that has been set to music. Isn't it simple to remember those verses as opposed to something out of Leviticus? I mean, I'm not hating on Leviticus, but there aren't a lot of songs being written about not eating the fat of an animal, wearing mixed fabrics, or the rules about circumcision.

At the risk of offending some preaching pastors, the truth is that people will, more than likely, never remember the points of the sermon preached on any given Sunday. After spending several hours throughout the week studying and preparing a message, most preachers don't even remember the points of their own sermons. That's why they have them written down in front of them on the pulpit. I dare you to ask your pastor to tell you what the points of his own sermon were last week. I bet he can't do it. Even though people most likely don't remember points of a sermon they heard this week, I am certain they can remember many of the lyrics their congregation sang together at the last worship gathering.

MUSIC AND COGNITIVE STUDIES

People remember song lyrics because melodies help us remember things. In the case of God's worshipers, melodies can help us remember His Word. Secular research supports this Biblical principle. Famed neurologist Dr. Oliver Sacks notes the connection between music and our ability to retain information. He points out this is not only the case in our modern time and culture: "Every culture has songs and rhymes to help children learn the alphabet, numbers, and other lists. Even as adults, we're limited in our ability to memorize series or to hold them in mind unless we use mnemonic devices or patterns—and the most powerful of these devices are rhyme, meter, and song."[4]

Likewise, cognitive neuroscientist Dr. Lutz Jancke also affirms

---

4   Oliver Sacks, *Musicophilia*, 237.

the effect that music has on our emotions and our ability to retain information. He speaks more specifically about the memory of events from the perspective of cognitive science. He states: "Because emotions enhance memory processes and music evokes strong emotions, music could be involved in forming memories, either about pieces of music or about episodes and information associated with particular music." He goes on to note the conclusions of many of his fellow researchers saying, "music is encoded in the brain by the perceptual memory system, which organizes auditory information into melodies and rhythms, rather than by the semantic memory system, which encodes meaning." Furthermore, he states, "If music has such a strong influence on emotions and our cognitive system, this raises the question of whether the memory-enhancing effect of emotional music can be used to enhance cognitive performance in general and in clinical settings."[5]

Dr. Sacks expounds upon his research in how music evokes emotion and memories in Alzheimer's patients: "The evocative power of music can be of immense value in people with Alzheimer's disease or other dementias, who may have become unable to understand or respond to language, but can still be profoundly moved—and often regain their cognitive focus, at least for a while—when exposed to music, especially familiar music that may evoke for them memories of earlier events, encounters or states of mind that cannot be called up in any other way. Music may bring them back briefly to a time when the world was much richer for them."[6]

Commenting on the nature of music, and how it has been used

---

5   Lutz Jancke, *Music, Memory, and Emotion*
6   Oliver Sacks, *The Power of Music*

as a therapeutic method among dementia patients, Alfredo Raglio states: "There are also the experiences of listening to music: music is potentially evocative, stimulates memories or states of mind through moments of verbalization after listening to music; further, music is used in order to facilitate the recognition of environments or structured moments of the day; finally, listening to music is used in the belief that it can effectively reduce behavioral disorders and enhance mood or socialization."[7]

Raglio continues to clarify the concept of music therapy among people suffering from dementia: "Music therapy is described as the use of music and/or of its components (sound, rhythm, melody and harmony) by a qualified music therapist, in individual or group relationships, in the context of a formally defined process, with the aim of facilitating and promoting communication, relationships, learning, mobilization, expression, organization and other relevant therapeutic goals intended to meet physical, emotional, mental, social and cognitive needs. The main finality of music therapy is that of developing potentialities and/or rehabilitating an individual's functions so that he/she might achieve an improved integration on the intro- and inter personal levels and therefore an ameliorated quality of life through prevention, rehabilitation or therapy."[8]

Secular research is catching up to something God has been telling us for generations. This is an old method, and neuroscientists are now beginning to see the powerful connection between music and memory, and hard data is proving this to be true. This research provides worship leaders with a very sobering reality:

---

7   Alfredo Raglio, *Music Therapy in Dementia*
8   Ibid.

We have a tremendous responsibility to feed Christ's Word to His sheep.

Alzheimer's and dementia patients may not remember their own children's names or faces, but they can still sing the words of hymns and worship songs that they have grown up singing all of their lives. After Sunday comes and goes, after our tenures at our churches are over, our influence can remain and continue to work in the hearts and minds of the people we serve long after the memories of most everything else fades away.

JOHN CALVIN'S APPROACH TO SINGING SCRIPTURE

The Reformers Martin Luther and John Calvin had a significant influence on congregational singing as we know it today. For centuries, congregational singing had become something that all but ceased to exist in most worship gatherings. Both of these faithful and courageous men of God brought congregational singing back to the people and made corporate worship more participatory, as God would have it, rather than a spectator's event.

Though Luther took a creative approach to worship by writing many original hymns, Calvin was stricter and believed that Christians should only sing the Psalms or songs taken directly from the words of Scripture, ensuring the lyrics would be divinely inspired as opposed to man-made and potentially heretical. These two perspectives on worship come from what are known as the normative and regulative principles.

The normative principle, which Luther ascribed to, teaches that any worship practice not specifically prohibited in Scripture is acceptable. Contrary to Luther, Calvin practiced the regulative principle, which is the belief that only worship practices specifically prescribed in Scripture are permissible.

Though many think of Calvin's approach to only singing Scripture a bit restrictive, it is admirable to know he was leading his congregation to sing God's words back to Him in worship. Calvin never had to worry about checking the theological content of his church's song lyrics, because they were singing songs written by the Perfect Lyricist. And what better worship language can we have than what God has already provided? John Stott notes: "God must speak to us before we have any liberty to speak to him. He must disclose to us who he is before we can offer him what we are in acceptable worship. The worship of God is always a response to the Word of God. Scripture wonderfully directs and enriches our worship."[9]

Most of us don't ascribe to the regulative principle, but no matter where we land on the discussion, it's hard to argue against singing God's own words in worship gatherings. There is no doubt Calvin's approach to congregational singing contributed to his congregants ability to commit large portions of Scripture to memory simply by singing it. It's a great thing to have creative lyrical expressions in our worship songs, but we must not neglect what God has already said about Himself. We can't write better songs than he has already written. Those with the gift of songwriting should use their God-given talents to write new songs for worship, but we must not forget that God is the greatest Songwriter. Use His lyrics. He's okay with us plagiarizing Him.

---

9   John Stott, *The Contemporary Christian,* 174.

SINGING SCRIPTURE

H.B. Charles notes: "Music in worship should be an extension of the ministry of the Word. Corporate singing and special music should serve to let the Word of Christ dwell in the saints richly. Let's be honest: as hard as we work on our preaching, people will remember the songs longer than they will remember our well-crafted sermon outlines. This should not embitter us. It should motivate us to make sure the music affirms and reinforces what we are teaching."[10]

As cool as it might be to think of ourselves as professional musicians, we have a much higher calling than that. I encourage all worship pastors not to consider themselves primarily ministers of music, but ministers of the Word who happen to use music as a means of ministry. We have a calling to communicate God's Words to people and to do what we can to feed the church as much of the Bible as we can. That is why singing Scripture is necessary if it is to remain in our hearts and minds.

One time I was hanging out with a few fellow worship leaders and I asked the question of what songs had their churches been singing lately. I wanted to get good song ideas, and find out what had been working in their local churches. We all shared songs that our congregations had latched onto and had been responsive to and we also discussed which ones hadn't quite worked. We talked about the songs from the previous Sunday, and I mentioned we sang "Everlasting God." Their response was, "Oh man! That's an OLD song." Which made me feel about as hip as Ned Flanders at a Jay-Z concert.

---

10   H.B. Charles Jr., *On Pastoring*, 138.

To call it an "old" song is laughable, but it is an older "new" song. I explained why I chose to lead my church to sing that song and will continue to do so. I don't do it because it's one of my favorite worship songs, because it is far from it. I don't do that particular song because it is hip and cool, because it no longer is. I don't add this song in my repertoire because people are begging me to sing it, because they don't. I use that song, and will continue to do so for this reason: it is Scripture set to singable music.

Isaiah 40:28-31 to be exact:

> *Have you not known? Have you not heard?*
> *The LORD is an everlasting God, the Creator of the ends*
> *of the earth.*
> *He does not faint or grow weary;*
> *His understanding is unsearchable.*
> *He gives power to the faint,*
> *And to him who has no might he increases strength.*
> *Even youths shall faint and be weary, and young men shall*
> *fall exhausted;*
> *But they who wait for the LORD shall renew their strength;*
> *They shall mount up with wings like eagles;*
> *They shall run and not be weary; they shall walk and not*
> *faint.*

When people sing, "Strength will rise as we wait upon the Lord (verse 31)…You are the Everlasting God…You do not faint; You won't grow weary (verse 28)…You lift us up on wings like eagles (verse 31)," they are singing God's very words back to Him and committing it to memory. How great is that? This song may not be hip or cutting-edge anymore, but God is glorified and the church is edified as they sing words from the Bible.

When tragedy strikes or hard times come to the worshiper, these truths of finding strength in our Everlasting God will be a comfort to his soul they will remember, in large part, because he sang the words in our worship gatherings.

I remember leading this song at a funeral for a friend of mine who tragically died in an automobile accident. Not only did the Scripture we all sang together minister to those hurting, but since then, when I hear of a tragedy, or I'm going through a difficult time, the fact that God is an Everlasting God comforts my soul. It reminds me as much pain and sorrow that exists in this life, it is only temporary. God is eternal and He rules over all things, even our tragedies. And one day, sorrow will be over when we, who have trusted in Christ, will spend life everlasting with our eternal God. He will renew our strength when we patiently wait on Him and trust Him to do so. Because I sang that song at a significant life event, the truth from the Scripture lyrics have stayed and will always stay with me.

To let "the word of Christ dwell in you richly" means God's Word is penetrating and residing in our hearts and minds. Setting God's words to music makes them memorable. I believe the faithful worship pastor should lead his congregation to sing songs that have Scripture texts put to singable music. If he has the ability, he should write relevant and easy to follow melodies to the Psalms so that his congregation can sing God's Words back to Him and be able to memorize them. These songs might not become big radio hits, but they will serve a better purpose for the church.

I would encourage all worship leaders to adopt this "what is learned in song is remembered long" philosophy. Teach your congregations to sing Scripture. Teach your children to memorize Scripture by making up little songs or jingles with the words of Scripture. It's extremely effective. So much so that people will learn, remember, and (hopefully) live in obedience to the Bible.

Worship leaders/music ministers are first and foremost ministers of the word. We are not simply musicians for hire. As a matter of fact, our musical abilities are secondary at best. Instead, we are pastors who teach God's Word, and we happen to use music as a significant vehicle to do so. We must plan our worship services, choose our songs, and write our lyrics as ministers who are trying to faithfully steward God's people and God's Word.

CHAPTER 2

SING LIKE TEACHERS

*"Let the word of Christ dwell in you richly, **teaching** and admonishing one another in all wisdom, singing psalms and hymns and spiritual songs, with thankfulness in your hearts to God."*

- Colossians 3:16

What was the first point of Christian theology you ever learned? For most it's probably of Christ's love for us. No doubt we learned this truth by singing songs like "Jesus Loves Me" or "Jesus Loves the Little Children." Before we even learned how to tie our own shoes, we can learn and comprehended the fact we are loved by Jesus. As little boys and girls, our Biblical understanding of God was being shaped because truth was being taught to us through songs that are simple and easy to remember.

In the last chapter we looked into Colossians 3:16 and saw how singing "psalms and hymns and spiritual songs" helps us commit Scripture to memory. The verse also notes that teaching is a result of Christians singing. What are we as worship leaders teaching through the songs that we choose to sing? Theology. We are teaching about the Person and works of our God, through the content of the lyrics. We teach of His attributes. We teach of His acts. When we sing in worship, we are retelling the Gospel story.

As a notable author and professor of worship, Constance Cherry states, "What is it that Christians sing? We sing the story of God. Worship is primarily a proclamation of the whole story of who God is and what God has done through His mighty acts of salvation throughout history."[11]

She goes on to say: "We sing because it is a vehicle for expressing our faith. The songs we sing testify to what we believe as Christians; they assert the doctrines of orthodox Christian belief and practice. Songs proclaim what we believe objectively, and in their singing we come to own that belief. Singing the faith helps to make it our faith. The repetition of melody and text embeds the meaning of the songs deep within us. We often find that those texts we repeatedly sing and are there to sustain us in the truth; their melodies and lyrics rise from a deep well within us and mysteriously re-present themselves when we need them most, sometimes even years later. The faith we sing is the faith that remains with us by virtue of song."[12]

This belief and practice of singing as a way to teach and re-

---

11   Constance Cherry, *The Worship Architect*, 153.
12   Ibid. 156.

inforce knowledge of the Word of God is nothing new. It is not a new concept that has been invented by modern worship leaders. Christian leaders are given many examples in Scripture where people used the tool of song to communicate the nature and works of God. As Tom Krueger notes, "Music is also used in Scripture to tell God's great works and, consequently, to stir up our faith. Musically etching the works of God into our memories causes these works to become more real to us."[13]

I think it is safe to say that no two people from the Old Testament were more used by God, as pertaining to worship, than Moses and David. They provide some incredible examples of how singing in worship has contributed to the theological shaping of God's people.

THE SONGS OF MOSES

Moses is, quite possibly, the earliest songwriter for God's worshipers. We know he is the first to write a psalm[14], and he is the first to write divinely inspired songs of worship. Moses' debut as a songwriter is recorded in Exodus chapter fifteen.

THE SONG OF THE RED SEA

When God demonstrated His great power and sovereignty over nature by parting the Red Sea and commanded Moses to lead the nation of Israel safely across dry ground the people were astonished. In that moment, the Scripture says they saw God's great

---

13 Tom Krueter, *Keys to Becoming an Effective Worship Leader*, 100.
14 Psalm 90

power and they "believed in the LORD and in His servant Moses."[15]

Not wanting the people to forget about what had just happened, Moses teaches the people the song that is recorded in the fifteenth chapter. This song was to be a reminder to the people who witnessed this nature-defying event of what God had done that day. It was meant to help the people recall how Yahweh proved Himself mighty and faithful. The song was to be taught to all future generations so that they could learn about that miraculous event and they too would be reminded of God's faithfulness that continues to all generations.

Being the first worship song we have recorded in Scripture, it is packed with truth that was taught to Israelites for centuries and still teaches us today. Not only does it recount the events that took place at the Red Sea and the deliverance of the Israelites, but look at the theology is within the song:

I will sing to the LORD, for he has triumphed gloriously; the horse and his rider he has thrown into the sea. The LORD is my strength and my song, and he has become my salvation; that is my God, and I will exalt him. The LORD is a man of war; the LORD is his name. "Pharaoh's chariots and his host he cast into the sea, and his chosen officers were sunk in the Red Sea. The floods covered them; they went down into the depths like a stone. Your right hand, O LORD, glorious in power, your right hand, O LORD, shatters the enemy. In the greatness of your majesty you overthrow your adversaries; you send out your fury; it consumes them like stubble. At

15   Exodus 14:31

the blast of your nostrils the waters piled up; the floods stood up in a heap; the deeps congealed in the heart of the sea. The enemy said, 'I will pursue, I will overtake, I will divide the spoil, my desire shall have its fill of them. I will draw my sword; my hand shall destroy them.' You blew with your wind; the sea covered them; they sank like lead in the mighty waters. "Who is like you, O LORD, among the gods? Who is like you, majestic in holiness, awesome in glorious deeds, doing wonders? You stretched out your right hand; the earth swallowed them. "You have led in your steadfast love the people whom you have redeemed; you have guided them by your strength to your holy abode. The peoples have heard; they tremble; pangs have seized the inhabitants of Philistia. Now are the chiefs of Edom dismayed; trembling seizes the leaders of Moab; all the inhabitants of Canaan have melted away. Terror and dread fall upon them; because of the greatness of your arm, they are still as a stone, till your people, O LORD, pass by, till the people pass by whom you have purchased. You will bring them in and plant them on your own mountain, the place, O LORD, which you have made for your abode, the sanctuary, O Lord, which your hands have established. The LORD will reign forever and ever.[16]

Imagine you were a young Israelite sitting on your grandfather's knee as he described what he saw that day when he himself was a little boy. As your grandfather began to sing the song that was taught to him by Moses, what truths about God would he be passing down to you, his grandson or granddaughter? What

---

16   Exodus 15:1-18

would you learn about God's character and nature based on this song? You would learn that God is our strength, our song, and our salvation (verse 2), He is glorious and powerful (verse 6), He is great and majestic (verse 7), there is no one like Him and He is holy (verse 11), He leads us with steadfast love and He is the Redeemer (verse 13), and He will reign forever and ever (verse 18).

When Moses finished singing, his sister Miriam followed his example. She gathered all of the women, those who fell under her particular circle of influence, and she began teaching them this song. Verse 20 says, "Then Miriam the prophetess, the sister of Aaron, took a tambourine in her hand, and all the women went out after her with tambourines and dancing. And Miriam sang to them: 'Sing to the LORD, for he has triumphed gloriously; the horse and his rider he has thrown into the sea.'"

Immediately after Moses finished the song, it is passed down to others. And we see Miriam singing the same lyrics that were given to Moses through divine inspiration. Notice how the words she sings in verse twenty-one, repeat what Moses began singing in verse one. The mention of Miriam is a picture of God's intention with this song in particular and with songs in general. God wanted truth to be passed down from generation to generation and the use of song will make it easier to do so.

The passing down of this song did not end with Miriam and the ladies she influenced. We are told in Revelation 15:3 that the redeemed saints that will be gathered around God's throne will be singing "the song of Moses." Just as God's people sang a song of being delivered out of bondage and being brought into the Promised Land, one day all the saints of God will sing a song of being delivered from spiritual bondage and being brought into rest in our eternal Promised Land. This should humble any songwriter. More than likely, none of the songs that we have written will last as long as this one.

THE SONG OF THE PROMISED LAND

Years later Moses would write another song for teaching and instructing the people of Israel (Deuteronomy 32). But this one would have a different intention. By this time, Moses was very old and the Israelites were about to enter the Promised Land. God told Moses he was about to die and that he was to bring Joshua into the tent of meeting so that God might commission him as the new leader of the Israelites (31:14). The Lord told Moses that after he would die, the people would fall back into sin and idolatry and He instructed Moses to write another song to teach and impart truth to the people that would be remembered for generations.

God said, "Now therefore write this song and teach it to the people of Israel. Put it in their mouths, that this song may be a witness for me against the people of Israel." (31:19)

He goes on to say, "when many evils and troubles have come upon them, this song shall confront them as a witness (for it will live unforgotten in the mouths of their offspring)." (31:21)

This song served as a reminder the Israelites belonged to the One True God and were set apart to serve Him and Him alone. It encouraged them to practice repentance and to strive after holiness. Did you catch the last part of verse twenty-one? It says the song will "live unforgotten in the mouths of their offspring." In other words, the truths of the song will be passed down to future generations and will dwell in their hearts and minds.

It is hard to forget songs. Just ask anyone who has watched a

Disney movie with their children. For me, it took months to get "Do You Want to Build a Snowman?" and "Let it Go" out of my head. Even a song that we have not heard for years, when it comes on the radio we can probably still sing along like we just listened to it yesterday.

The truths about Who God is and what He has done by delivering the Israelites out of slavery would be a constant reminder to this generation and were to be passed down to future generations. When Moses finished teaching them the song he said to them, "Take heart all the words by which I am warning you today, that you may command them to your children, that they may be careful to do all the words of this law." (32:46)

Imagine being an Israelite. You have finally made it to the Promised Land. God has kept His promises and remained faithful to you and it is painfully obvious you have not been and are not being faithful to Him. The words of this song Moses taught you long ago nags at your soul, reminding you of the character and nature of God. It evokes memories of what He has done for you. There are also many times the song leads you to repentance and God uses it to draw you back to Him. This was God's design for Moses' song and His intention for the worship songs that we sing today.

THE LEGACY OF DAVID

No other name is as synonymous with worship through song as David the shepherd, the king, the songwriter, the worshiper. And for good reason. He was the writer for more than half of the Psalms—seventy-eight to be exact. How many of us musicians can say we have written any song that will stand the test of time, much less, seventy-eight of them that have been used for worship for several millennia? He also played the harp and entertained the king (1 Samuel 16:23). How many of us have ever had such a prestigious gig? Not me.

David also understood his responsibility as a musician and his calling to be a singing teacher. He understood the powerful role that music played in shaping people's thoughts of God and how music could be used to impart truth and how God could use it to implant His Word into the hearts of people. The Psalms that he wrote reflect this understanding. In particular, Psalm 119 which is by far the longest psalm (with 176 verses)—it is a song specifically about God's Word.

This understanding and passion for the role music plays in worship and our sanctification fueled David's ministry. One of his greatest accomplishments was being responsible for organizing musicians and singers to be used for worship. He first did this when they moved the Ark of the Covenant to where the temple would be built (1 Chronicles 15:11-16). This event was to be celebratory with great rejoicing of what God was going to do, and serve as a reminder of how God had proven Himself faithful in times past. David also took this opportunity to use music as a way to ingrain truth into the hearts of the people. He appointed some Levites "to invoke (record/remember), to thank, and to praise the LORD, the God of Israel." (1 Chronicles 16:4) He assigned some to play harps and lyres, Asaph to play the cymbals, others to play trumpets and David appointed them to sing this "record" of thanksgiving as a way to remind the people that their God was a faithful God and to remind them of His great deeds and works. (1 Chronicles 16:4-36)

Look at some of the lyrics of the song. The singers sing that we are to "MAKE KNOWN his deeds" (verse 8); "TELL of all his wondrous works" (verse 9); in verses twelve and fifteen, it instructs the people to "remember" and in verse fifteen, it commands them to "Remember His covenant forever, the word that He commanded, FOR A THOUSAND GENERATIONS."; "TELL of his salvation from day to day" (verse 23); "DECLARE His glory among the nations..." (verse 24). The prophet Isaiah grew up singing the words of this song and even repeated verse twenty-four as an adult (Isaiah 66:19). It's obvious the intent was to communicate a message. It was meant to teach the people history of their people and theology of the God they worshiped. The intent is once again to be sung and passed down and to teach future generations who God is and what He has done. The Hebrews are told to not only pass it down to their children and grandchildren, but they are to be missional with the song.

David's son Solomon, who would be his successor to the throne, probably grew up with many memories of his dad sitting down with an instrument, working on a new song. This had a profound impact on him and he inherited his dad's songwriting ability. He was the author of eighteen of the psalms. He also wrote fourty-two odes, which were not divinely inspired Scripture, but were songs containing sound theology. Solomon, like David, understood why God gifted him with such an ability. When the temple was built under Solomon's reign, much like his dad before him, when the Ark of the Covenant was being placed into the temple, Solomon organized the musicians and singers to lead the people in the praise and worship of their God. 2 Chronicles 5:11-13 records:

And when the priests came out of the Holy Place (for all the priests who were present had consecrated themselves,

without regard to their divisions, and all the Levitical sing-
ers, Asaph, Heman, and Jeduthun, their sons and kinsmen,
arrayed in fine linen, with cymbals, harps, and lyres, stood
east of the altar with 120 priests who were trumpeters;
and it was the duty of the trumpeters and singers to make
themselves heard in unison in praise and thanksgiving to
the LORD), and when the song was raised, with trumpets
and cymbals and other musical instruments, in praise to
the LORD, 'For He is good, for His steadfast love endures
forever.

Like his dad, Solomon appointed musicians to lead in worship and celebration. They sang and played musical praises when they brought the Ark of the Covenant to the same place—the place where the temple would one day stand. David's band was celebrating what God would do and Solomon's band was celebrating what God had done.

What would it have been like to be an Israelite on that day? Hebrew men, women, and children were privileged to see and hear such a magnificent worshipful experience. No doubt the singers and musicians sounded incredible. It was an experience that would stay in their hearts and minds for the rest of their lives. We know they never forgot because years later, when the temple was destroyed and the people were in captivity by the Persians, God's people remembered the truths of this song. When they were allowed to return to their homeland they remembered the song as they made the long journey. And once they rebuilt they foundation to the new temple, they organized the musicians and singers like Solomon and David, and they worshiped.

And when the builders laid the foundation of the temple of the LORD, the priests in their vestments came forward with trumpets, and the Levites, the sons of Asaph, with cymbals, to praise the LORD, according the directions of David king of Israel. And they sang responsively, praising and giving thanks to the LORD, 'For He is good, for His steadfast love endures forever... (Ezra 3:10-11)

The Israelites were gathered together again once the temple was completed (Nehemiah 12:27-47). Through the power of song, truth was passed from generation to generation. The words of this song not only taught each generation the story of how God worked in, through, and for the nation of Israel, but it also helped shape what they believed about God. This song helped to remind them the LORD is "good," and "His steadfast love endures forever."

Have you ever noticed how many times this phrase is repeated throughout Scripture? It's used over 200 times. This simple lyric is packed with theology, and was used to teach generation after generation about an incredibly important aspect of God's character and nature: that He is good and that He has love. And not only is He loving, but His love is STEADFAST. It is a steadfast love that ENDURES. And His steadfast love doesn't just endure temporarily, but it endures FOREVER!

THEOLOGICAL ACCURACY

Looking into these ancient examples that are given to us in Scripture, it should humble our spirits and sober our minds as it relates to our calling and responsibility to God and to the people we lead. Paul's instruction to young pastor Timothy is a charge not just to preaching pastors, but also to worship pastors: "Keep a close watch on yourself and on the teaching. Persist in this, for by so doing you will save both yourself and your hearers." (1 Timothy 4:16)

As influencers and theology shapers, we are accountable to guard the theological accuracy of the songs our congregations sing together. Warren Wiersbe says, "A singer has no more right to sing a lie than a preacher has to preach a lie. Our singing must be theologically orthodox as well as technically adequate. No amount of beautiful harmony can atone for theological heresy."[17]

Knowing that music is an effective tool for shaping one's theology, it is important to understand a person can be trained in theology that is either sound or flawed. Therefore, worship leaders must be diligent in checking the theological content of their songs and making sure the lyrics are biblically accurate. Mark Dever states: "Jesus uses His Word to build or edify the church. So it makes sense that we only sing songs that use His Word both accurately and generously. The more accurately applied scriptural theology, phrases, and allusions, the better because the Word builds the church, and music helps us remember that Word, which we seem so easily to forget."[18] We, as worship leaders, must ask ourselves: Are we committed to being a singing teacher of the truth, the whole truth, and nothing but the truth?

Just because a song is popular, or is musically appealing, doesn't mean it is a theologically accurate song. I think about

---

17   Warren Wiersbe, *Real Worship*, 115.
18   Mark Dever, *The Deliberate Church*, 84.

John Lennon's song "Imagine." Musically speaking, it's a beautifully written song. I just wish so strongly wish the theology wasn't so flawed. Check out the first verse:

> *Imagine there's no heaven, it's easy if you try*
> *No hell below us, above us only sky*
> *Imagine all the people living for today*

For years I have been not only a worship leader, but a secular musician as well. I have had many requests to play this song and have even been tempted a time or two to do so. But, as a follower of Christ I can't, in good conscience, sing a song that is contrary to the truths I am called to share with the world, even though it is still an incredibly popular song, and has a beautiful and catchy melody. I simply can't communicate a message that denies the reality of heaven and hell and calls people to only live for the moment with no concern for eternity.

I believe my worship leader friends would agree with me. We wouldn't sing a song in a secular setting that conflicts with the Bible. Why would we do the same in a worship setting? You like a song that you hear on the radio? You sing a song because your other worship leader friends are doing it? You lead the congregation in a song because many of the people are requesting it? My question is: What is the song saying and does it jive with Scripture? It doesn't matter how popular it is, what sentimental attachment you or others may have to it, or how musically appealing it may be. If the theology is inaccurate you need to pass on it. There are too many great songs available to us today to be singing theological garbage.

Stephen Miller notes: "When we are leading our people in worship through singing, we are actually putting words into their mouths to sing to God. Therefore, it is imperative that we guard with all diligence the songs that we choose for our people to sing and be careful to maintain the doctrinal integrity of the content we are teaching. It must be truth in song every time. No exceptions."[19] Let that reality sink in. Reflect on the incredible responsibility we are entrusted with. We are to be good stewards of the truth, the people we lead and influence, and the praises we lead them to sing.

THEOLOGICAL DEPTH

The first question we must ask ourselves when discerning which songs to choose for our congregations is: Do the lyrics teach truth? The second question we must ask is: Do the lyrics teach ANYTHING? A song might not possess theological inaccuracies, but that doesn't mean it contains theology. It might be so shallow it's not saying anything at all.

The Christian music scene of the 90s has not aged well. Though it was an important time in our history of how the modern worship movement has progressed, I don't want to revisit most of the songs that came out of that era. No offense to the songwriters. I appreciate how God used them to pave the way for worship musicians today. We owe them a huge debt of gratitude. But many of those songs didn't teach much about the God we worship. Many of them have been dubbed "seven-eleven" songs: we sing the same seven words eleven times.

I think about the song "I Could Sing of Your Love Forever."

---

19   Stephen Miller, *Worship Leaders, We Are Not Rock Stars*, 73.

Is it just me, or did it literally feel like we were going to sing it...
FOREVER?! To be fair, this isn't just a modern praise and worship problem. Remember the song "When the Roll is Called up Yonder"? Check out these theologically rich lyrics:

> *When the roll is called up yonder*
> *When the roll is called up yonder*
> *When the roll is called up yonder...(wait for it)*
> *...When the roll is called up yonder, I'll be there.*

Now, don't get me wrong. Repetition has a purpose and simplicity has it's place. Some of the Psalms were written in a simple and repetitive manner. There is something beautiful in simplicity, but our souls can't be healthy without a sufficient diet of robust theology. Don't let overly simple and repetitive songs be the main dish of the theological meal that you are feeding your congregation.

A good rule of thumb when writing worship songs or putting together a worship service is to imagine a person coming into a worship service with absolutely no knowledge of the character of God and the work of Jesus Christ. Based on your song choices, how will that change for that person when the worship service is over? Will their theology still be as undeveloped as when they came in? Or will the songs lead them to know something about Who God is and what He has done for them? To be clear, I don't believe that God would have us to shape our worship services to cater to the lost. I believe the church's worship gatherings are specifically for the gathered believers. But, my question still stands. You will have young believers that are incredibly new to the faith and have very little knowledge of God and Christ. Will they walk out of your worship gatherings with a deeper understanding of their Lord?

Gordon Fee once said, "Show me a church's songs and I'll show you their theology." If Gordon were to walk into your church this Sunday, what would he perceive was your church's theology? Would he be able to tell? Would he think your church believes in heresy? Would he think your church believed in anything at all? Or, would he observe a church that has a passion for knowing God and making Him known? Our songs are meant to teach. Let's make sure the songs we choose are capable of teaching because they actually say something that testifies the greatness of the Person and Work of God.

CHOOSE SONGS LIKE YOU ARE PLANNING A SERMON SERIES

Like a pastor plans a sermon series based on specific needs in the congregation during certain seasons, or what he may want his congregation to know about God, I believe the worship pastor should do the same kind of planning. Much like Bob Kauflin's "Twenty-Year Rule" which asks the question: Based solely on the songs they sing, what do I want my congregation to know about God after twenty years under my leadership?[20] This kind of forethought and intentionality should be a significant part of the teaching ministry of the worship pastor.

In order to plan worship services like a sermon series with the purpose to teach and instruct worshipers in theology, I would charge the worship planner with four tasks in accomplishing this. First, I would encourage them to make use of the Christian worship calendar. Some churches and denominations are more litur-

---

20   Bob Kauflin, *Worship Matters*, 119.

gical by nature than others. For those like me, who are not from a background that uses the Christian calendar regularly, this can still be a useful tool in planning out worship services. You may not even want to use the entire calendar. Perhaps you might use it during the Advent or the Easter season. Either way, the Christian calendar can give you a great outline and road map for what songs, doctrines, and themes your church will be singing and learning about throughout the year.

Secondly, I would encourage worship leaders to sing the attributes of God and the gospel of Christ. For certain times of the year, the worship pastor may want to lead the congregation to focus on a specific attribute of God that they will sing about in one day. For example: one week your song themes may be centered around God's love. The next week may be focused around His grace, His mercy, His sovereignty, etc. This approach can provide you with several weeks of themes and song ideas in which to teach your people about Who God is and what He is like. The worship planner may also intentionally thread the story of the gospel (sin, the cross, the resurrection) throughout his/her worship songs. This requires intentionality and careful planning on the part of the worship pastor, but I believe will reap good fruit from the Gospel seeds that are sown.

Thirdly, I would urge worship pastors to use a variety of song genres. I do not necessarily mean musical genres, though that could keep things fresh and creative. What I mean is to imitate the pattern that Paul laid out in Colossians 3:16 by singing "psalms and hymns and spiritual songs." Though there has been some debate as to the specific meaning behind each of the song types, I believe the point is to use many different kinds of songs. This variety will help accomplish the goals of teaching, admonishing, and having the word reside in your heart and mind.

DOCTRINAL NEGLECT IN WORSHIP SONGS

There is a trend in churches where certain Christian doctrines that are essential to the faith, and essential to certain denominations, that are being neglected, avoided, or forgotten. In Lavon Gray and Frank Page's book, Hungry for Worship, they discuss this trend as a "Loss of Theological Distinctiveness."[21] They note that since we have such a broad selection of song resources, we are utilizing songwriters from various theological persuasions. Though this broad selection of songs is great because there are some phenomenal songs are being written by people who aren't in my particular Christian denomination, it does present challenges and creates what Gray and Page describe as a "Theological Melting Pot."[22]

For generations, the use of hymnals has served to teach and train congregations in their core theological beliefs. Denominations had their own hymnals compiled with hymns that taught doctrines were specific to them. For my denomination, the Southern Baptist Convention, it was The Broadman Hymnal, and later The Baptist Hymnal.[23]

Though my church doesn't use a hymnal, and I would prefer that we not, we use songs from all kinds of writers (Chris Tomlin, Hillsong, Isaac Watts, etc.). I think this is a healthy trend on one hand, because we have so many songs to choose from, we have

---

21   Lavon Gray and Frank Page, *Hungry for Worship*, 123.
22   Ibid. 123.
23   Ibid. 121

no reason to ever sing junk. But I also think the theological discernment of worship leaders and pastors should be on full alert. We need to be aware of what we are feeding (or not feeding) our congregation through the songs we sing.

Ask yourself: What doctrines would my people learn if it was solely dependent on the songs I lead them in?

Also ask yourself a more sobering question: What doctrines would be lost if it were solely dependent on the songs I lead them in?

Some of the doctrines I hold firmly and are largely not being written about today are the doctrine of the Security of the Believer, the Trinity, and the Deity of Christ.

I believe the reason for this shift is when songs are written with the intention of appealing to as many people as possible, certain doctrines are neglected to ensure potential consumers aren't alienated. I have no problem with these songwriters we are using, and I thank God for them. I'm grateful they are able to make a living that way, but we should also be discerning with the songs that are being released to the public. It's okay to use songs that aren't on the radio, or the CCLI top 100 (though there are great songs to be found that way). On the other hand, if we have to use more obscure artists/songwriters in order to lead our congregations to sing a more well-balanced theological diet, then so be it.

CHAPTER 3

SING LIKE THEOLOGIANS

"Show me a church's songs, and I'll show you their theology."

–Gordon Fee

It troubles me a little when I hear a Christian state they are not a theologian. Perhaps theology scares them. Maybe they don't feel competent enough in that area to accept such a title. Either way, it drives me INSANE when I hear a pastor, worship leader, or any other kind of church leader make that statement. In a sense, I understand what they mean. They are not theological giants like R.C. Sproul or John Piper. I understand. Most of us are not gifted with minds like that. But, here's the deal: EVERYONE IS A THEO-LOGIAN. It's not a matter of whether you are or aren't one, it's a matter of whether you are a good one or a bad one.

Theology simply means the study or knowledge of God. We all have things we believe about the Almighty. Some of those beliefs are true, some of them are false, and some of them are incomplete, but we all have them nonetheless. It feels silly to state those responsible for teaching theology (through song) must be theologians, but it is necessary. The fact is, as leaders...as Christians, we have a responsibility to try and be the best theologians we can possibly be.

Choosing theological ignorance is a very serious crime against the Lord. Hosea said of Israel: "My people are destroyed for lack of knowledge; because you have rejected knowledge, I reject you from being a priest to me." (Hosea 4:6) Granted, none of us are choosing to neglect growing in our theology because we don't love God. Most of us neglect it because we feel inadequate. If you feel this way, you are not alone. Bob Kauflin said, "Studying doctrine and theology is hard. Becoming a good theologian is harder than learning a new riff, and initially not as much fun."[24]

Even though it's difficult to be a good theologian, we have a responsibility before God to know Him and to make Him known. No matter how great our musical skills are, if we aren't good theologians, we can't be the worship leaders God has called us to be. Likewise, without good theology, we can't be the WORSHIPERS God has called us to be. Kauflin states, "Regardless of what we think or feel, there is no authentic worship of God without a right knowledge of God."[25]

This is a topic I am very passionate about. I personally believe while musical training is important for worship leaders, Biblical

---

24   Bob Kauflin, *Worship Matters*, 29.
25   Ibid. 28.

training is far more crucial to our ministries. My educational journey led me to receive training in theology, but not in music. Perhaps my opinion of this matter is due to being a little self-conscious about being a music minister with no formal musical education or training. But, I have to believe that there is truth to my perspective on the matter. God has called us to be competent theologians. The good news is, everything He calls us to, He is willing and able to give us the tools and ability to follow through in obedience.

THEOLOGICAL GATE-KEEPERS

Paul tells the young pastor Timothy to "Keep a close watch on yourself and on the teaching. Persist in this, for by so doing you will save both yourself and your hearers." (1 Timothy 4:16) This is a command that applies to all of us who are entrusted to shepherd Christ's flock. Even though we are not completely responsible for what every individual in our churches believe, we do have significant influence over the Body of Christ. Ultimately, they have to study Scripture and listen to what the Holy Spirit is teaching them. We church leaders are oversee the lyrical content that is presented to the church. For those who lead congregational singing, we keep a "close watch" on the teaching by keeping a "close watch" on the songs we select.

Worship Pastor, Dr. Lavon Gray notes the role of a worship pastor as that of a "theological filter."[26] He says, "Bible-based theology is foundational in our roles as church leaders. Its role is exponentially expanded as planners of worship because the songs we

---

26   Lavon Gray and Frank Page, *Hungry for Worship*, 133.

select shape how others view God."[27]

To be a theological gate-keeper for our church requires that you have discernment. This is a quality grossly lacking in American Christianity today. False teachers are given a platform because people can't discern the truth from a lie. Instead of calling out false teachers and teachings, we give them a platform, book deals, speaking tours, and packed arenas. In many circles any attempt at being biblically discerning is criticized as being judgmental and self-righteous. Even in the music ministry world, movements like Bethel Music and their angel feathers and gold dust (seriously... look this up) are influencing Christians all over the world.

I think that the reason for the rise of false teaching in America is because Christian leaders either lack spiritual discernment themselves, or the back bone to call out false teachers and teaching, or maybe a little of both. Either way, the church will never authentically worship as God deserves to be worshiped, if it is not passionately pursuing and growing in robust theology.

Stephen Miller says, "The songs we sing teach us theology. For better or worse, as worship leaders, the songs we choose to sing with our churches will inevitably shape the way they view God and interact with Him. Songs that are rich with gospel truth and weighty in God-centered, Christ-honoring content will shape worshipers who understand and adore God, while deficient, flimsy, man-centered songs will produce a lack of understanding of who God actually is, which leads to deficient, flimsy, man-centered worship. If we are to worship God, we must know who He really is."[28] (Miller, 71-72) He continues: "We must drench our worship

---

27   Ibid. 133.
28   Stephen Miller, *Worship Leaders, We Are Not Rock Stars*, 71-72.

in doctrine and saturate our services and songs in Scripture. In doing so, we will lay a strong theological foundation on which the Lord will build His kingdom. He will be lifted up and draw men to Himself."[29]

As a whole, the church will never grow in its theology if we as Christian leaders, aren't leading by example and aren't able to properly feed and care for their souls with Biblical truth. Church members should feel confident in coming to us, not just the preaching pastor, with theological questions. We also have to give them reason to be confident in us. We have to be trustworthy in our understanding of the Scriptures. The church needs a worship leader that has a love for and a discipline in studying the Scriptures and knowing God more deeply.

PROPER SONG VETTING

To be a good singing theologian, to guard the church against singing false doctrine, and to feed the church by singing sound doctrine, the worship planner must be intentional with vetting the worship songs are used in their weekend worship gatherings. Every church and worship leader's vetting process will look different because every local church has a specific worship culture with unique leaders with their own set of skills, gifts, and personalities. Still, it is important to establish some method of properly vetting the songs are selected for corporate worship. Here are a few things I believe will be helpful in this area:

ASK THE RIGHT QUESTIONS

When choosing songs for worship, the wrong questions are

---

29   Ibid. 76.

often the ones that are asked, such as: Is this a popular song? Does it have a good, memorable melody? Have people requested it? Is it one our church loves and has sung for years? To be fair, some of the right questions are asked, but they can often be asked after the fact.

The first question I would suggest asking is: Does this song teach TRUTH? It doesn't really matter how beautifully the song may have been written, or how well-known it may be, or what kind of sentimental attachment people may have to it; if the lyrics don't communicate truth, then it should not be sung.

The second question worth asking is: Does this song teach ANYTHING? The song may not necessarily have false doctrine in it, but does it have ANY doctrine in it? Is it theologically shallow? If you truly want to be a singing teacher, there must be content and substance in the songs you are singing.

Thirdly, I would ask: WHO is the hero of the song? Is the song man-centered or Christ-centered? Does the song speak of the character, nature, and works of God or does it speak more about what we do, say, feel, etc.?

Fourthly, I would ask: What is your church's theological IDENTITY? Today we have thousands of songs to choose from and they come from dozens and dozens of sources, all of whom have varying theological convictions, some of which may conflict with you and your church. I think all of these different sources are incredible, and I thank God worshipers everywhere can worship with songs from various backgrounds and denominations, but it is worth noting that it should cause us to pay attention to how we are serving and shaping the theological identity of our own local Body of believers.

Fifth, it should be asked: "Is this one of the BEST choices that

I can make? With all of the incredible song options that are available to us today, there is no reason for the church to ever have to sing songs that are sub-par. With the thousands upon thousands of worship songs at our disposal, worship planners should be choosing nothing but the best of the best. Occasionally, I may tweak a song lyrically, because I don't like the way a certain line is phrased, be it grammatical or theological, but if I have to tweak a song's lyrics too much to make it "better," then I'll scrap it and use another song in its place. Let's not settle for less, but go for the greatest songs that will stand the test of time and will best serve our congregations.

This obviously is not an exhaustive list of questions that should be asked, but these are enough for you to grasp the point and to get headed in the right direction. All songs should face scrutiny before we present them to our congregations and use them as tools for discipleship.

GATHER A TEAM

Along with asking the right questions, I believe it would be useful to gather a team to help answer those questions. There are many benefits to working with a team as opposed to working alone. Jesus often paired up or grouped the disciples when assigning them a task. Proverbs 11:14 says, "Where there is no guidance, a people falls, but in an abundance of counselors there is safety." The truth is, we are better when we work together.

Working with a team will help us see blind spots. Our team members will offer a different perspective that will cause us to notice things we probably wouldn't have recognized by ourselves. Working with a team allows people in your ministry to observe and learn your heart and passion on the matter of theological integrity.

When you are working with a song-vetting team, this can lead to discipleship and gospel conversations. When discussing a song's lyrical content, this will naturally cause people to dig into the Scriptures and discover truths about God and the gospel they haven't known before, and it will reinforce the truths they already believe in. This model of song-vetting will also help gauge if the lyrics are understandable even if they are of sound theology. It may reveal areas that require some teaching and explaining from the platform, such as what an "Ebenezer"[30] is.

No matter what this may look like for you in your local ministry, there will be great benefits to recruiting and working with a team. Your ministry will be stronger. Your relationship with those on the team will be stronger. And the church as a whole will be stronger.

NETWORK WITH OTHER WORSHIP LEADERS

Similar to recruiting a team within your church to help with song-vetting, it would be useful to have the voice of other worship leaders as well. This can provide space for helpful dialogue on what songs other worship leaders are doing. You can exchange thoughts about certain songs or lyric. This can be a platform where worship leaders can discuss lyrical red flags. I think it is important for church leaders not to view each other as competition, but as co-laborers. Though we may work at separate churches, we are all working for the same Kingdom.

I would caution though, when deciding on a network of wor-

---

30 From 1 Samuel 7:12 and the song, *Come Thou Fount*

ship leaders, one should choose wisely. Not every worship leader has the biblical knowledge and discernment, or places a high enough priority on theology, or has close enough theological convictions for this kind of conversation to be beneficial.

I know of one guy that was part of a network of worship leaders in the area. He thought it was a safe place to have discussions like this. He was wrong. He brought up the song "What a Beautiful Name" by Hillsong. Now, I think most people who have heard this song agree that it's a great song. There has been some discussion about the first line of the second verse which states: "You didn't want heaven without us." Is that an untrue statement? No. But, I share this leader's concerns (along with many others) that the lyric didn't quite seem to fit the rest of the song. The rest of the lyrics are incredibly Christ-centered, but that one lyric seems to turn the focus away from Jesus and make us the center. It was the worship leader's thought that the way that line was written seemed to conflict with God's perfection, as if He NEEDED us. It was just a concern that he wanted to bring up and have some healthy dialogue about, but it backfired. There was no place for that within that network of leaders. That meeting didn't go well for him, and relationships, as far as I know, were damaged.

I would encourage all worship leaders to first network with other co-laborers and help each other properly vet their church's worship songs. And secondly, make sure it is a network of people that are trusted to be theologically competent, humble in spirit, and have the same passions you do about wanting to disciple and teach the church through theologically robust and accurate songs.

TRUST YOUR PASTOR

I know several pastors who openly admit they know nothing about music. This causes them to have to extend a great deal of trust to their worship leader. There are a couple of potential problems that may come as a result of the non-musical pastor being "hands-off" when it comes to the music ministry of the church. First, the pastor may be too self-conscious to approach the worship leader about song and lyric quality. And secondly, the worship leader may grow too comfortable functioning with very little pastoral input, resulting in defensiveness when the pastor does step in and questions a song's lyrical content.

Let me say the pastor should be concerned with the lyrics the church sings and the worship leader should be humble enough to value and submit to the pastor's insight. I know worship leaders who want a line clearly drawn in the sand, so the pastor worries about only the sermon and the worship leader worries only about the music. This is not right. Ultimately, the pastor is the lead shepherd, and his leadership should be followed.

While worship leaders have a responsibility to be the theological gate keepers through song selections, senior pastors have the responsibility to be the theological gate keepers in every area of the church. If the pastor has concern about a song or lyric, then there is good reason to dialogue and come to an understanding of his concern. You and the pastor are on the same team, trying to accomplish the same goals. Don't be defensive or take it as a personal attack when he has a theological problem with a song, even if it's one you've written. Chances are, even if he's not musical, you might glean some great ideas from him.

God has entrusted us with the truth. In order for us to be good stewards of it, we must consistently strive to grow in our love for and knowledge of the Scriptures. People should and will look to us for theological leadership. How are you leading them? What are you teaching them about the God they worship?

If you feel ill-equipped to fill the role as one of the lead theologians in your church, work hard at changing that. Be a student of the word. Be mentored. Read good books...not any books...GOOD books. You are going to give an account for how well you shepherded the hearts and minds of your congregation. You must be a theologically capable leader. But the good news is, YOU CAN DO IT. God wants to be known by you. He doesn't want His characteristics and His ways to be a secret. He wants to reveal them to us, that's why He has given us the Bible. God is with you in this journey.

I am encouraged by the resurgence of theologically-driven worship leaders, conferences, books, etc. But, there is still room for improvement. We are to be life-long learners of Christ. If you desire to be, He will lead you to grow in being a very capable theologian, so you can help others to know Him and make Him known.

CHAPTER 4

SING LIKE PROPHETS

*"Let the word of Christ dwell in you richly, teaching and **admonishing** one another in all wisdom, singing psalms and hymns and spiritual songs, with thankfulness in your hearts to God."*

-Colossians 3:16

B ob Dylan has been a hero of mine for years. I named my first son after him. I think Dylan is one of the greatest songwriters to have ever lived. He certainly is one of the most important songwriters in American history. In the early 1960s this shy, fresh-faced Minnesota kid, barely into his twenties became known as "the prophet of a generation." He earned this title because he helped give a voice to young people, spoke out against injustices, and helped change the course of history with nothing but his guitar, harmonica, and songs.

One of his more famous songs, "The Times They Are-A Changin'" spoke out against the politicians that were preventing forward thinking and positive change:

Come senators, congressmen, please heed the call
Don't stand in the doorway, don't block up the hall
For he that gets hurt will be he who has stalled
There's a battle outside and it's ragin'
It'll soon shake your windows and rattle your walls
For the times they are-a changin'

He also sang to those who refused a change, warning them that the culture will evolve, and people can either be part of a constructive progression or be left behind:

Come mothers and fathers throughout the land
And don't criticize what you can't understand
Your sons and your daughters are beyond your command
Your old road is rapidly agin'
Please get out of the new one if you can't lend your hand
For the times they are-a changin'

His second release, The Freewheelin' Bob Dylan, became his breakout effort. In this album, he established himself as a counter-cultural songwriter, especially with issues of racial discrimination with songs like "Oxford Town." This song told the story of James Meredith, the first black person to enroll as a student at the University of Mississippi in the city of Oxford. Because of this, a riot broke out injuring many and killing two. Dylan offered commentary on the event which shed light on the injustices that were happening at the time:

He went down to Oxford town
Guns and clubs followed him down
All because his face was brown
Better get away from Oxford town

Oxford town around the bend
Come to the door, he couldn't get in
All because of the color of his skin
What do you think about that, my friend?

There's no doubt that lyrics like this helped to eventually put an end to segregation. This is one of the songs that reflected his convictions, which quickly led him to one of the most significant gigs in American history: The March on Washington.

On August 28, 1963 Martin Luther King gave his famous "I Have a Dream" speech on the steps of the Lincoln Memorial in front of 250,000 fellow civil rights supporters. This became the most important moment in the Civil Rights Movement. This was at a time when white men never shared a microphone with black men, but Dylan (along with others) broke down that race barrier and stood united with their African-American brothers and sisters. Together they sang like Old Testament prophets, declaring the injustices of their nation, calling it to repentance, and proclaiming hope for a better future.

Dylan's words set the stage for Dr. King's iconic speech. First, he sang "When the Ship Comes In" which is a song of longing for a day when justice will finally arrive. The song is filled with biblical imagery and references of when good triumphed over evil, a foretelling of days to come in America. Next, he sang "Only a Pawn in Their Game." This song tells the story of the 1963 assassination of civil rights leader Medgar Evers. The song also speaks of how whites have been indoctrinated with and enslaved to a racist way of thinking and living. He reveals how, at that time, the poor southern white person was living under oppression as well, except his oppression came from a society of politicians and leaders who wanted to preserve their white supremacist way of life.

Bob Dylan's final song, and possibly his most famous, "Blowin' in the Wind," was not sung by him, but by folk trio Peter, Paul and Mary. Dylan's prophetic lyrics asked timely questions such as:

How many roads must a man walk down before you call him a man?
How many years can some people exist before they're allowed to be free?
How many times can a man turn his head and pretend that he just doesn't see?

There is no doubt his music had a significant voice that day in changing our nation for the better. Dr. King himself closed his incredible speech by quoting song lyrics from an old black gospel song: "Free at last! Free at last! Thank God Almighty, we are free at last!"

Though Bob Dylan was not a prophet like Isaiah or Jeremiah. He did not write new books of the Bible, nor give us fresh revelation from God. However, he happened to live in a time when songs were used in a prophetic way. They called our nation to observe our sin and repent of it. His songs played a huge role in reshaping the hearts and minds of the people in this country. Dylan's words taught people to love their brothers and sisters of all colors. His lyrics charged white people to not remain silent when they see injustice being done to a person of color. His songs reminded people, in a sense, that we are all created equal and are made in the image of God.

Songs can move a nation.

OUR RESPONSIBILITY AS "PROPHETS"

In First Samuel 10:5, when Saul was to be anointed as king, we are told of a group of singing prophets. Scripture says, "As soon as you come to the city, you will meet a group of prophets coming down from the high place with harp, tambourine, flute, and lyre before them, prophesying." Later on, when Saul's successor, David organized the musicians and singers to be used as worship leaders, First Chronicles 25:1 notes some men "who prophesied with lyres, with harps, and with cymbals." These days, modern worship leaders and musicians will not be called to the office of "prophet" because the cannon of Scripture is now complete. We have no need for a new revelation. As a matter of fact, cults are formed when leaders rise up, claiming to be prophets with a NEW revelation. So, when I think of speaking and singing like a prophet, I think of proclaiming God's truth with passion and conviction.

Author Nathan Corbitt put it this way: "Musical prophets stand on the edge between the sanctuary and the street and provide a vision of God's future reign. Music is prophecy when it leads people to truth and justice. Music is not a fortune-telling device, but a sonic tool that foretells future consequences based on present realities. At times, this musical truth lies outside the boundaries of a just and righteous kingdom. Yet at other times, it is the voice of the kingdom to an unjust world."[31]

This idea of "musical prophet" causes me to think again about Colossians 3:16. It says, "...admonishing one another..." To admonish means to warn, reprimand, urge, or advise. All of these are characteristics that are found in God's prophets. If the songs of the modern church are to be used to reprove the saints, they should have elements that are prophetic in nature. They need elements that quote and reference Scripture, communicate the nature of God and the works of Christ, and stir the church "to love and good works."[32]

Most of us will never have an opportunity quite like the one that was presented to Dylan on that iconic day when he and 250,000 others marched for freedom. But, no matter what setting

---

31   Nathan Corbitt, *The Sound of Harvest,* 82.
32   Hebrews 10:24

we are called to, or how many people we are allowed to influence, we must be aware of the prophetic nature to our calling as Christian worship leaders. There must be, to some extent, a dimension of admonishment to our congregational singing. Worship pastors should make intentional steps in their worship planning and songwriting to provide their congregations with a balanced diet of songs. One of those necessary elements are songs that call us to action and/or repentance.

WHY MUSIC IS AN EFFECTIVE TOOL FOR PERSUASION

Andrew Fletcher, a Scottish politician famously said, "Let me make the songs of a nation, and I care not who makes its laws." Why did he say this? Is this philosophy true? Keep in mind, this guy was someone who was on the front lines societal change. He was appointed to be an influencer of his culture. Even though he had political influence, he knew that the real guidance comes from the arts, specifically, through songs. Although he and his colleagues penned laws, he was well-aware of the fact that the law-makers can be swayed by the power of a musical message.

This still rings true in modern times. I grew up listening to musicians that tried to use their talents as a platform for social change. Rappers like Tupac and NWA rhymed about police brutality, racism, and poverty among the black community and Rock bands like Rage Against the Machine and U2, and songwriters like Bob Marley and Bruce Springsteen have all offered social commentary through their songwriting and have used their platform to spur on changes in society. The opinions and convictions of these legendary musicians live on and grow in the hearts of their fans in a more powerful way than if another legislator were to say the identical things from behind a podium reading from a teleprompter. Why? Because of music's prophetic nature.

I think music is effective at persuading people because melodies, beats, and rhythms all cause us to let our guards down to the message within the lyrics. We are more apt to listen to a song in which we disagree with its message, than if we were to listen to a verbal presentation from someone with differing views than ours. Music makes a message easier to receive. It makes to more palatable and convincing.

Nathan Corbit muses on the nature of music and how it conditions the heart and mind to receive and respond to admonition: "Music softens our messages in a way we could not or would not dare attempt with words. Because it is indirect, the hearer has a way out—a way to save face and maintain the relationship—rather than having to respond directly and risk open conflict. Many Westerners who value problem solving over the maintenance of relationships often miss the subtleties of music meditation. Reared in a 'what you see is what you get' culture, they prefer to fight for the truth of the moment with harsh words, thus risking a loss of redemptive resolution. While it takes patience and perceptual alertness to decode the messages of mediating music, it is a valuable skill for understanding. When conflict is unattained, however, music's greater power inspires people to action."[33]

I also think music is persuasive in nature because it incites our emotions and connects them to the message of the song. Corbit notes: "Music has real power to motivate. It calls for and creates an emotional response in humans. When combined with words, it

---

33   Corbitt, 89.

can have a powerful effect on the hearer. At first your emotions are jolted by the sounds you hear. Then you make a choice. If you like the music, you then explore the meaning of the text. If the words make sense and have meaning to you, then you begin to internalize the music."[34]

Earlier I mentioned Bruce Springsteen. He has a song called "Johnny 99" which is about a guy who got drunk, shot and robbed someone, was arrested, and sentenced to ninety-nine years in prison. If I were to have a simple face to face conversation with Bruce about this guy, and Bruce were to try to get me to empathize with Johnny, it probably isn't going to happen. Johnny chose to rob and murder an innocent man, a man who was working hard trying to provide for his now widowed wife and orphaned children. But, when we listen to the song, Bruce makes us realize the regret that Johnny carries. How he fell on hard, desperate times by losing his job. He was drowning in debt and was on the verge of losing his home. This led him to make the terrible decision to rob an innocent man. The song makes us realize the anguish Johnny's mother felt as the judge announced his nearly a century-long sentence, and as the bailiff was about to take this mother's son to jail where he will spend the rest of his life.

At the end of the song, one begins to (or at least I do) empathize with "Johnny 99." What makes us want to see things from the desperate perspective of this guy? The fact that his story was told through a song. Because the music captures the emotion of the moment. It connects our hearts to the character of the story. Because it grasps our hearts, it changes the way we think about the situation.

---

34   Ibid. 118

PROPHETIC SONGS IN WORSHIP

If our songs are going to be prophetic in nature, if they are going to admonish the worshipers, it will require that they call us to repentance, holiness, obedience, and action. Unfortunately, this is a lyrical quality that is scarce today. I did a study of the lyrical content and themes of the worship songs are found on the CCLI top 100 list. At the time of this writing, only four of them had any kind of admonishing qualities. The only criteria I had for considering a song to be one of admonition was for it to have only one line that called the worshiper to some sort of action. Only four percent of the most frequently sung modern worship songs had this quality in the lyrics.

A recurring theme I did find, however, was a "God's on your side! You can do it! You slay those giants, you child of God, you!" kind of stuff. The reason there are so many songs being written like that is because there is a huge market and appetite for it. Entire Christian music radio stations have slogans that advertise being uplifting and encouraging. To be fair, we as believers, and as Christian leaders, should be positive and supportive. Many people we come in contact with desperately need to be encouraged. But, they also require a balanced diet. Often times people need to be shaken up. We need songs that are going to make us aware of injustice, sin, idolatry, and apathy. Our souls must have songs that will charge us to repent of those things and join in the fight against them. Songs that will break us, not just hug us are essential. That is what will ultimately encourage and strengthen us.

Now, I'm not saying that these kinds of songs aren't being written, though that might be the case, I am saying these songs aren't being sung in our churches. If we are to fully obey Colossians 3:16, and model our approach to congregational singing after it, this will take an intentional effort on our part as worship planners, singers, and songwriters because congregational songs that have admonishing qualities are hard to come by nowadays.

This hasn't always been the case though. I encourage you to grab a hymnal. If you are younger and need a definition, a hymnal is a book that had a bunch of old songs in it. Instead of chord charts, they were filled with lines (called a "musical staff") and weird shapes (representing musical notes). I'm only kidding, but if you were to look in a hymnal, it contains many songs of admonishment. Some songs like "Brethren, We Have Met to Worship" have a charge for evangelism; "Break Out, O Church of God" calls the church to care for the poor; "Stir Your Church, O God, Our Father" is a song encouraging the worshiper to live a missional lifestyle and to have a social conscience. And many songs like "Just as I Am" or "Only Trust Him" called people to repent of their sins.

Songs that had prophetic content or admonitions were very common throughout Scripture. Look at Psalm thirty-seven, for example. In this Psalm alone, there are seven points of admonishment:

"Fret not yourself because of evildoers; do not be envious of wrongdoers!" (verse 1)
"Trust in the LORD, and do good." (verse 3)
"Commit your way to the LORD; trust in him, and he will act." (verse 5)

"Be still before the LORD and wait patiently for him." (verse 7)

"Refrain from anger, and forsake wrath!" (verse 8)
"Turn away from evil and do good." (verse 27)
"Wait for the LORD and keep his way..." (verse 34)

In this one Old Testament worship song, there are far more admonishments than what we can find in an average worship song today. What does this call us as worship leaders to do today? I believe this calls us to a great amount of intentionality. Why? Because of the lack of songs to choose from with this quality in them. We are in a time where we have seemingly countless songs available to choose from, and there are so many incredible songs that we should be singing. The problem is, admonishment is often a neglected quality in today's worship songwriting. Be intentional. Dig around and mine for this gold. If you can't find any, then write some yourself if you have the ability. Who cares if your songs never get put on an album or on Christian radio? You are called to serve your local congregation and God will equip you to serve them in a way that is faithful to His Word.

Songs of admonishment and singing like a prophet are key elements in shaping the theology of the church. It reminds us of His holiness, righteousness, and justice, and his expectations on us as believers to follow and obey him, to turn from sin, and to love and minister to mankind with a gospel service. So, let's do it! Let's move our church...our nation...through the power of singing truth.

CHAPTER 5

SING LIKE EVANGELISTS

"...do the work of an evangelist..."

-2 Timothy 4:5

One Sunday morning after leading the congregation through "Jesus Paid it All" as a closing hymn a man named Marty, who served as an elder at my church, came up to me. This was not unusual, as Marty often came up to me after a service and encouraged me and told me what a great service it was and how much he appreciated my family and me. But this particular Sunday, he told me that "Jesus Paid it All" was his favorite hymn. He then proceeded to tell me how God used the words of that song to reveal to him his need for a Savior and to put his faith and hope in the finished work of that Savior. He further told the story of his conversion which will forever serve as a reminder to me of the importance of leading a congregation in worship through singing, and what is at stake every single week.

Marty was born with significant hearing problems, in a time when the technology to improve his hearing simply didn't exist. Marty was essentially deaf. He came from a family that was faithful in bringing him to church each week and his mother served as the church pianist. As long as he could remember, he sat in the pews as his pastors preached the gospel. He went to Sunday school, Vacation Bible School and other Bible activities for children, but never was able to hear well enough to know what was going on or what was being said. Despite his handicap, each week while his mother played the piano, a man in the church would bring him up and sat him next to his mom so that he could hear the piano while he held a hymnal in his lap. While Marty sat with his mother on one side, the man sat next to him on the other. With one hand on Marty's shoulder the man sang closely into Marty's ear, and with the other hand, he pointed to the words that were being sung so he could follow along.

Marty was never able to hear a sermon being preached, or a Bible-lesson being taught, but he heard the Gospel through songs. And God used this incredible tool of music and the faithfulness of his mom and a kind-hearted man to be good stewards of that tool, and he used it to draw Marty to trust in Christ. Marty has lived a life of faithfulness to the Lord and to His church and it's because of the Gospel that was played and sung to Him.

This song has always been used to help shape the beliefs about God among people who follow Him. The same logic can be used for those who do not yet know God. While they are singing, or hearing truths about God and His Gospel, their hearts and minds too will be shaped and molded. How many little boys and girls, teenagers and adults are hearing the life-changing message of the

Gospel of Christ being sung to them each week? It may be the preaching pastors or the evangelists that get the privilege to lead someone to pray to receive Christ while we stand behind them on the platform leading the invitation songs, but make no mistake about it, God uses the truths that are in the songs that we sing to draw people into a saving knowledge of Christ. This is how we begin to shape the theology of the church. We sing the gospel, in order for those who are not part of Christ's church YET will begin to have their hearts and minds shaped with the truth about Him.

SONGS AND CONVERSION

Harold Best once said in his book, Music Through the Eyes of Faith, that "the gospel must be sung, not just preached."[35] For many generations, worship music has been used by God to draw the lost to salvation through the Gospel. From Moses to Paul, the Scriptures are filled with examples of how songs were used to communicate Who God is and what He has done. Best goes on to say: "Witness music is effective. It works. People are moved to repentance and drawn to Christ. And why not? If the gospel is the power of God unto salvation and if the gospel is sung, it follows that the power of God will be made manifest in the midst of its singing."[36]

The connection between song and conversion is nothing new. Psalm 96:1-3 says, "Oh sing to the LORD a new song; sing to the LORD, all the earth! Sing to the LORD, bless his name; tell of his salvation from day to day. Declare his glory among the nations, his marvelous works among all the peoples!" Why do you think this charge of evangelism was written into the Divinely inspired

---

35   Harold Best, *Music Through the Eyes of Faith*, 204.
36   Ibid. 205.

worship song? I think it's to remind God's worshipers that we are to live, preach, and SING the Good News of Christ to those who do not know and love Him yet. Imagine being a Hebrew worshiper singing this Psalm on the Sabbath. As you are singing the words, you are reminded that you are surrounded every day by people who don't know or follow the One True God. The words of the Psalm stir your heart and give you a burden for the lost. This is God's design.

In Acts sixteen, we see a phenomenal story of how singing has been used in the conversion of the lost. In this chapter, Paul and his ministry partner, Silas, have been arrested for preaching the Gospel. Something incredible happens one night as they are in a Philippian jail. Verse twenty-five says, "About midnight Paul and Silas were praying and singing hymns to God, and all the prisoners were listening to them." Gospel seeds were planted in the hearts of the people in the jail as they heared Paul and Silas singing the Gospel all night. After that, there was a great earthquake which opened all of the doors (verse 26). Just then, the jailer ran into the jail and saw the doors were all opened, he was about to commit suicide. He wanted to take his own life because, according to Roman law, if a prisoner escaped, the prisoner's sentence was to be carried out through the guard on duty. This guy believed taking his own life was better than the torment he probably would receive.

But God had a better plan for his life. Paul called out to the guard not to take his life. He showed the guard that they were all still in their cells. This hardened prison guard was shaking like a leaf. There is no doubt that this earthquake gave validation to the truths that were being sung in that jail that night. As a result, the guard came to know Christ and so did his family at home. (verse 34.

Church history has many examples of faithful saints who shared the Gospel, won the lost, and reproduced more worshipers of God through the truth being presented in their worship leading. Martin Luther is one of these people. He was responsible for the resurgence of congregational singing during the Reformation. According to Towns and Whaley, Luther was convinced he won more converts through his singing and songwriting than he did through his sermons.[37] They also note the ministry of John and Charles Wesley as missional worship leaders/songwriters:

> By mid-century, hymns were consistently being used in worship—especially in rural and less aristocratic communities. Hymn writers strategically used hymns as a means for communicating theology and doctrine. For the first time, music was used as a tool for evangelism, as people began singing in public songs of personal experience—an important innovation to worship. Hymn writers of the seventeenth and eighteenth centuries were concerned with composing songs that expressed both doctrine and personal experience.[38]

Worship leaders have a heritage of being stewards of truth through the content of their songs. As a preacher must be faithful to preach the gospel accurately and thoroughly in his sermons, the worship leader must be faithful to preach the gospel accurately and

37   Elmer Towns and Vernon Whaley, *Worship Through the Ages*, 108.
38   Ibid. 126.

thoroughly in his songs. In *Unceasing Worship*, Harold Best emphasizes this point when he said:

> If the gospel is the power of God unto salvation, then God in his power will make sure that the readied hearer is not left in the dark and the inherent hearer will be urged into further maturity. The secret is not in talking baby talk to the unredeemed and adult talk to the converted, nor in seeking a happy medium between the two so as to conform to eased-up protocols of certain kinds of seeker sensitivity. The secret lies in the authority, the conviction, the unswerving bluntness of all truth preached, sung and written.[39]

LEADING WORSHIP WITH THE LOST IN MIND

Before I expound on this, let me be clear. I believe the corporate worship gathering of the church is meant for those who are already believers. Unconverted people cannot worship God, because they have not yet come to trust in Christ. But, the truth is, the worship leader must function as an evangelist and there must be an evangelistic quality to the content of his ministry. We would be naive at best, to think that there aren't lost people in our congregations. To fail to acknowledge the fact that there will be unregenerate people in our gatherings and to feel no responsibility to sing the gospel to them would make us bad stewards of the people God has brought to our churches to be under our influence.

---

39   Harold Best, *Unceasing Worship*, 80.

If worship leaders are to lead worship with the lost in mind, the question is: HOW? How does the worship pastor "do the work of an evangelist" while leading worship from the platform? I would suggest five ways.

The first way is to be intentional with the song choices. Like the teaching and admonishing aspect of the worship leader's role, this requires the worship leader to listen carefully and critically to song lyrics and to plan strategically, as well. He must remain mindful of the people attending worship gatherings—whether live or through online or televised services—who do not know Christ. The worship planner should write and/or choose songs that call the lost to repentance and a saving knowledge of Jesus Christ.

Secondly, the worship pastor must be intentional with his spoken words. During moments like this, the leader can explain the meaning of song lyrics and worship practices during the service. This would be helpful for all members of the congregation, both long-time and new, but especially for those present who have not trusted in the gospel and know very little of God's Word.

The third way that the worship pastor can function as an evangelist through congregational singing is by using culturally relevant music. When utilizing the MUSICAL language of the lost people in that local culture, the worship pastor is speaking a CULTURAL language of the people in that community, which will make them more receptive to the LYRICAL language of the song. This will likely improve the receptivity of the gospel and the fruitfulness of the worship pastor's ministry in this area.

The fourth way the worship pastor can do the work of an evangelist is through production of excellent music. Excellence can include the content of the song lyrics, as well as the production and presentation of the music. The Scriptures demand that music be done with skill. Psalm 33:3 says, "Sing to him a new song; play skillfully on the strings, with loud shouts." Not only is it unbiblical for worship music not to be excellent and skillful, but it will be a turn off to non-Christians and outsiders. Christians who are consistent participants in a local congregation's worship gathering have a way of being more forgiving of bad music. Honestly, we as the church tolerate sub-par music more than we really should. We will excuse it far more than non-Christians will. Excellent music will help a person be attentive to the message of the song, while poor music will distract from it.

And finally, the worship pastor can host and/or produce intentional music events. He or she can host a traveling Christian artist, or produce a local gospel concert. He should also make significant effort to embrace the arts, in particular, the art of live music. The church should not be the enemy of the arts, but a champion for them. As messy as it may be, the worship pastor can function as an evangelist to the artistic community by supporting and contributing to local music.

WORSHIP AS WITNESS

A failure to fulfill the calling worship leaders have as Gospel stewards produces terrible results. Worship based on emotionalism is not sustainable, nor does it reap life-changing, soul-saving results. It is not based on Truth. In Can't Wait for Sunday, Michael Walters says, "Worship is meant to strengthen and enhance the witness of God's people in the world. The weakness, ineffectiveness, or absence of the church's witness indicates a disconnect between worship and life that must be mended. If it is not, the result will be worship that is perfunctory and, ultimately, powerless."[40]

Sally Morgenthaler notes:

> Our worship of God either affirms or contradicts our message about God. Unbelievers (including those who are churched and unchurched) will draw lasting conclusions about the veracity and uniqueness of our God based on what they see or do not see happening in our weekly church services. Do they detect something supernatural and life-changing going on? Can they sense God's presence and work among us? Are they experiencing something in our midst they have never seen before?[41]

Worship is not a means to an end though. As Franklin Segler said, "Worship is an end in itself; it is not a means to something else. When we try to worship for the sake of certain benefits that may be received, the act ceases to be worship; for then it attempts to use God as a means to something else."[42]

Because this is true, worshipers don't worship (or use worship) so they can become better evangelists or missionaries. The final goal in everything they do is to make more worshipers of God. In Let the Nations Be Glad, John Piper said, "Missions is not the ultimate goal of the church. Worship is. Missions exists because worship doesn't. Worship is ultimate, not missions, because God

---

40   Michael Walters, *Can't Wait for Sunday*, 198.
41   Sally Morgenthaler, *Worship Evangelism*, 9.
42   Franklin Segler, *Christian Worship*,

is ultimate, not man. When this age is over, and the countless millions of the redeemed fall on their faces before the throne of God, missions will be no more. It is a temporary necessity. But worship abides forever."[43]

Therefore, worship leaders: SING THE GOSPEL. The saved need to hear it. The lost need to hear it. Your eternal impact does not end when the Sunday morning benediction has been given. We are planting good Gospel seeds in the hearts of those we are singing with. Because of this, we should plan intentionally, worship passionately, sing with conviction. Sing like an evangelist and trust the Gospel to do its good work of salvation.

---

43   John Piper, *Let the Nations Be Glad*, 11.

CHAPTER 6

SING LIKE SHEPHERDS... NOT SHOWMEN

"For years and years I chased their cheers, the crazy speed of always needing more. But when I stop and see you here, I remember who all this was for."

–The Greatest Showman, *"From Now On"*

"He must increase, but I must decrease."

–John 3:30

A number of years ago, I was invited to be in an awkward situation. A couple of small, rural churches wanted to get together and hold a "revival." I don't believe true revival can happen simply by scheduling it on a calendar and declaring it to be, but that's beside the point. I was invited to lead worship at this series of gatherings because the churches wanted someone to "come and do some contemporary praise choruses" in order for them to "draw in the young people." I knew instantly I was going to fit in about as much as Al Bundy at a black-tie affair.

I was asked to come meet with the planning committee for this event to help them bounce ideas around and that's when I met the piano player. When I was first asked to lead worship, I was told it would be just me, alone with my guitar. I quickly realized she had inserted herself into this situation and now this gig was going to be a piano and guitar duet. I figured this out when she introduced herself as the one who plays every single service. I agreed to it, simply because I was a guest, and I'm a team-player...or maybe I'm just too much of a chicken to speak my mind.

A few weeks later, I showed up for the first night of the "revival" to a building that reeked of old church carpet smell, had no sound system, no projection, the floor squeaked loudly every time someone made the slightest move, and to my astonishment (not really), there were no "young people." Needless to say, it didn't feel like I was selling out Madison Square Garden.

As I suspected the piano was horrendously out of tune. It probably hadn't been serviced in years. Even despite the piano players choppy playing style, no sense of tempo, and inability to read a chord chart, this was going to make playing with her simply impossible. After several minutes of trying to figure out how these two instruments were to work together, I finally made the call to do the congregational songs myself and have the piano play the prelude, offertory, and a postlude. In my mind, I was still attempting to use her, but from her perspective, it wasn't good enough. It offended her that she wasn't going to play during the congregational songs like she did "every Sunday for thirty-seven years."

As the night progressed, the churches had also brought in a southern gospel trio to sing several songs. They were "professional" enough to bring their own sound system, which they didn't bother sharing with me. Between every song they all three (in unison), chugged water from their water bottles...you know...like the pros do. I'm all for keeping the vocal cords hydrated, but I don't need that much water if I'm performing in the desert. The trio's showcase singer was much younger (mid 40s), with gelled hair, and ripped jeans (the kind that you buy that way/the kind that the kids wear). He didn't move his mouth much when he sang and when he hit the high notes, it sounded like nails on a chalkboard, but he acted like he was Bon Jovi.

After the piano-queen and the Bon Jovi trio began the speaker, who spoke more about himself and his spiritual accomplishments than the finished work of Jesus. By the end of the week, it was clear that Jesus wasn't the hero of the preacher's sermons, but it was the preacher himself.

I learned a valuable lesson that week in an incredibly humble setting. It doesn't matter how lowly the situation may be, there will always be people who are consumed with using the platform as a chance to exalt themselves. It's a serious problem in music ministry and Christian leadership. In fact, it's an epidemic. It's something each one of us must be ready to fight and kill when we feel it swell inside us.

ROCK STAR WORSHIP SYNDROME

This is what Stephen Miller calls the "Rock Star Worship Syndrome." He notes: "We've seen him--the messy-haired rocker worship leader or the neatly coiffed music director. Either way, though, he wants to be a rock star, to make himself the center of worship."[44]

This problem is present everywhere in Christian church circles. We find it in churches of every style and size. In our flesh, all worship leaders crave recognition and making much of ourselves. It's essentially the same thing the Serpent tempted Eve with, to "be like God." (Genesis 3:5) There is something about being on a platform or stage, leading others and getting a response from them, and then receiving compliments afterward that jacks with our minds and hearts. We must always fight against it and keep that in check.

To be fair, it's not just the fault of the worship leader. Many churches crave the rock star. They want the show and the flash. They want to be entertained. That's the reason many worship leaders in their forties and fifties are suffering from ageism. They get fired—even though they have many fruitful years of ministry left in them—only to be replaced with a younger, hipper (though less experienced) worship leader. Many pastors also want the flash and the show a rock star brings because it keeps people happy and the email inbox free of complaints. These cravings for entertainment and show come straight from our flesh and the fact we simply don't believe Jesus is enough.

This is a trend that MUST STOP. Worship leaders are called to be shepherds, not showmen. It's not our job to "WOW" our congregations with our vocal or musical talents, but to shepherd them, and to shape their hearts and minds to the things of God. Being a singing teacher requires a lot more humility. It's not as glamorous, lucrative, or often times, affirming as being a showman, but it's

44   Stephen Miller, *Worship Leaders, We Are Not Rock Stars*

much more satisfying, and reaps eternal rewards.

JESUS THE GOOD SHEPHERD

No one provides us with a better example of being a humble shepherd than the Good Shepherd, Jesus. He, being the second person of the Trinity, left His glory behind to be born into this world, to serve and to save undeserving people.

He summed up His mission to earth in Mark 10:45 when He said, "The Son of Man came not to be served but to serve." One of the ways He demonstrated this to be true was when He washed the feet of the disciples. While Jesus had His disciples gathered in the upper room, they observed the annual Passover meal and He instituted what's known as "The Lord's Supper."

After the meal, Luke 22:24-27 records there was a debate—which was frequent among them—about which of the disciples was the greatest. Jesus responded by saying, "Let the greatest among you become as the youngest, and the leader as one who serves. For who is the greater, one who reclines at the table or one who serves? Is it not the one who reclines at the table? But I am among you as the one who serves." Upon saying this, He stooped down and washed their feet which by the way, in that culture, was a job for the lowest servant.

While all of these entitled schmucks were debating about how awesome they were, God in the flesh stooped down and humbly washed the toe-jam off their nasty, crusty, muddy feet. The next time you sense your pride swelling up within you right before you take the stage on Sunday morning, or when people flood you with compliments on a job well done, think about this image.

The apostle Paul provided a similar admonishment when he

said, "Do nothing from selfish ambition or conceit, but in humility count others more significant than yourselves. Have this mind among yourselves, which is yours in Christ Jesus, who, though he was in the form of God, did not count equality with God a thing to be grasped, but emptied himself, by taking the form of a servant, being born in the likeness of men. And being found in human form, he humbled himself by becoming obedient to the point of death, even death on a cross." (Philippians 2:3, 5-8)

This passage of Scripture speaks of the Kenosis, which means the "self-emptying" of Christ. If the King of kings chose to make himself nothing, why in the world do we think we are so great? If the God-Man can lay His life down, why, in our flesh, do we seek to exalt ourselves? Why would we use our gifts, talents, and platform God gave us to glorify Himself, and try to glorify ourselves? Aren't you glad Jesus chose to be a humble shepherd? He didn't have to be. He wasn't under any obligation to be born into this world and die for our sins. Instead, He made a good and merciful and HUMBLE choice to do so.

JOHN THE BAPTIST

I've always admired John. Even though he wasn't a worship leader, his characteristics remind me of what a worship leader is and should be. In some ways, the modern hipster worship leader models John perfectly. They both have eccentric behavior. John lived in the wilderness and called people to repent of their sins. Some young worship leaders still live with their parents and blog about the problems of society. They both are on peculiar diets. Where John ate locusts and wild honey, hipster worship leaders want gluten-free, organic, vegan, etc. They both have interesting fashion choices. John wore camel's hair and modern worship leaders wear skinny jeans and (even in the summer) scarves and beanies.

Although I make these comparisons in jest, there are some great qualities about John I think all of us who lead God's church in worship should strive for. His entire reason for existence was to point people to Christ. Long before he was born, Isaiah prophesied about John's role in God's plan: "A voice cries: 'In the wilderness prepare the way of the LORD; make straight in the desert a highway for our God.'" (Isaiah 40:3) John knew it was him Isaiah spoke about (John 1:23), and he took his role seriously and fulfilled it passionately. When Jesus came to John to be baptized and to begin his public ministry, John declared: "Behold, the Lamb of God, who takes away the sin of the world!" (John 1:29) After all of the preaching and ministry work he had done, ultimately he wanted all eyes to be on Jesus.

John 1:35-36 recorded something counter-cultural to our modern way of thinking about ministry: "The next day again John was standing with two of his disciples, and he looked at Jesus as he walked by and said, 'Behold, the Lamb of God!' The two disciples heard him say this and they followed Jesus." This is counter-cultural because many churches and ministry leaders view each other as competition instead of co-laborers of the Gospel. Why? Because they are functioning like showmen and not as shepherds.

Most ministry leaders have faced this from time to time. We spend a great amount of energy investing into people (as a whole and as individuals) and we see them leave our church and go to another one down the street. Let's be honest, that hurts. And that's also normal.

Notice that John wasn't territorial when two of his disciples left to go follow Jesus. John didn't think, "Hey! I've been the one out here in the wilderness, preaching every single day and gathering this group of people. Who does my cousin Jesus think He is to just swoop in here and steal my disciples?!" John had spent a great amount of time and effort in preaching, ministering, and accumulating a following. None of that mattered to him when Jesus showed up. He wanted all attention to be on Christ. That's why he was doing ministry. John's words in John 3:30 perfectly sum him up as a person and what his mission in life was, "[Jesus] must increase, but I must decrease."

Our purpose is to point people to Jesus, to grow HIS following, not OUR following. We are to humbly instruct people about the character and nature, the Person and work of Christ. Through the songs we sing, the words we speak, the prayers we pray, and the Scriptures we read, we are shaping the hearts and minds of believers towards the things of God. This will never happen if we are more concerned about people being captivated by us and wowed by our talents than by being captivated and wowed by Jesus.

So, worship leader, are you seeking to serve or be served? Our role is to shepherd people in their worship of God and to help shape their thoughts and beliefs about how great God is, not about how great we are. If the only thing you have taught people during your ministry is that you are a great musician or singer, then you have failed. You have wasted opportunities that were entrusted to you, if your congregation has not learned from you something about the attributes of God, the gospel of Christ, and how to live a life that reflects and brings glory to our Lord.

CHAPTER 7

SING LIKE CARETAKERS

"Sing with me, just for today. Maybe tomorrow, the good Lord will take you away."

–Aerosmith, *"Dream On"*

Imagine Jesus in His final moments here on earth. He had been conspired against, falsely accused, betrayed, humiliated, and beaten nearly to the point of death. As He hung on the cross, He suffered major blood loss, dehydration, exhaustion, trauma, agony, and the sorrow of the Father turning away from Him. The Scriptures don't tell us, but I wonder what was going through His mind during those six hours of being crucified. Did He think about you and me? Probably. Did He try to stay focused on eternal paradise to try and cope with the pain? I know I would have. I wonder if

He reflected on childhood memories. I think it's a great possibility.

Scripture records Jesus saying seven different things while being crucified. All of them are significant, but I find two of them particularly interesting for those of us who lead worship in song. Jesus quotes lines from two of the Psalms. Matthew 27:46 records Him saying, "My God, my God why have you forsaken me?" This is a direct quote from Psalm 22:1. Luke 23:46 notes Jesus speaking again to God when He said, "Father, into your hands I commit my spirit." This being a line that was taken from Psalm 31:5.

This is important for us as worship leaders. While Jesus was in agony, in the final moments of His earthly life, He reflected back on songs that He had sung in worship since He was a young boy, worshiping in the temple. While his life faded away, he found those song lyrics to be a source of comfort during this time. We only have seven things we know Jesus said during these six hours, and two of them came directly from songs.

Though there is something to say about the worship pastor ministering to a dying saint with his physical presence, that is not always possible. I believe worship pastors minister to people in this season of life and death through the songs they lead their congregations to sing. Where the music minister's physical presence may not always be available, his influence can still remain. There are many ways our songs minister to people in their final moments in life. The truths we lead our congregations in singing can stay with them forever and will quite possibly be used to comfort them in their final moments and to shepherd them from this life into the next.

PLAN WORSHIP WITH THE DEATHBED IN MIND

Scripture is clear there will come a day when every earthly life will pass away. Hebrews 9:27 states, "It is appointed for man to die once, and after that comes judgement." Christians know the answer to the question of what awaits us after death. For believers in Christ, it is the Good News of eternal life. But the process of death can still be a painful and scary process. Part of the worship leader's duty is to pastor those saints who pass from this life into the next, when that time inevitably comes. James 5:14 notes the pastoral responsibility to minister to those who are sick and dying, "Is anyone among you sick? Let him call for the elders of the church, and let them pray over him, anointing him with oil in the name of the Lord."

Zac Hicks notes worship pastors must essentially function as morticians: "As worship planners and leaders, we need to think about how we can present this vision of the future in a way that speaks to the very real and present fears we all bring into worship. The metaphor of a mortician, as odd as it sounds, is helpful here. Good morticians are skilled in the caring art of preparing bodies for burial. I believe that a worship pastor is a mortician for the body of Christ, on who faithfully prepares the church for her encounter with death, not as a final experience of defeat, but as a transition into life everlasting."[45]

Similarly, John Witvliet says, "Christianity is nothing if not a way of thinking about death."[46] We as teachers and worship leaders must use our influence to shape a healthy perspective of death as well as help people build a strong foundation for when that time

45   Zac Hicks, *The Worship Pastor,* 135.
46   John Witvliet, *Worship Seeking Understanding,* 291.

comes.

Death is something all clergy must face at some point in their ministries. It is an element of pastoral ministry that cannot be avoided. Significant ministry happens around hospital beds when the pastor is counseling and praying over a dying saint. But the worship pastor has a unique opportunity to shepherd those into the next life through the songs he teaches and leads. Hicks states: "When we talk about heaven in our worship, we need to confront the truth about death. This might seem like a depressing question to think about, but it is necessary to ask: Is there room for death in our worship songs, prayers, readings, and transitional words? The answer we find in the Psalms, the worship and song book of the church, is unequivocally yes."[47]

The example of Jesus on the cross shows us in a person's dying moments, songs of worship may come to mind to bring them comfort and to reassure the saint of what is waiting for them on the other side of death. Songs of worship have been used to comfort the dying in many scenarios. Sometimes it's a dying saint whose mind is still sharp, but the body is failing, and the only thing that comforts them is the assurance of Christ. Other times it's in Alzheimer's patients who might not be able to recognize the names or faces of their children or spouse, but they can still sing the words of hymns they grew up singing. It may often be when families are called in to gather around a loved one who is moments away from slipping into eternity, and the family joins hands and sings hymns and songs of praise together. Make no mistake about it worship leader, our worship songs help to comfort during times of death.

What should this call worship pastors to do? I would say that

---

47   Hicks, 136.

a worship pastor should have a long-term vision for their ministry. They should keep in mind that their influence goes far beyond the Sunday morning worship service. Long after the worship gatherings are over, the songs the worship pastor teaches and leads will stay with people all of their lives. We don't need to lead worship with a momentary momentary Sunday-morning perspective, we need to lead worship with the death-bed in mind.

PLAN WORSHIP WITH ETERNITY IN MIND

The fact that worship songs comfort the dying calls for the worship pastor to evaluate the content of his song choices. Will these songs comfort dying saints and their families when they are passing from this life to the next? What do they say about eternal security, God's character, or the finished work of Christ? More specifically, what about eternity is being said in the songs?

The book of Revelation gives us examples of songs with an eternal perspective. Chapters four, five, and seven record the songs of future praise. Revelation 15:3-4 records a song of future deliverance: "Great and amazing are your deeds, O Lord God the Almighty! Just and true are your ways, O King of the nations! Who will not fear, O Lord, and glorify your name? For you alone are holy. All nations will come and worship you, for your righteous acts have been revealed." These songs of future worship give us hope in the face of death.

What about the songs of today? Do we sing about heaven much anymore? Decades ago, particularly in southern rural churches, Christians sang out of the Heavenly Highway Hymns. Though, with some exceptions, much of the theology of this hymnals is pretty shallow and man-centered, and could even be flirting with making heaven into an idol. Even with those circumstances, the saints from that era had a firmer grasp on eternal paradise than we do today. The reason for this is because they sang about it all the time.

I've been to many funerals in my time of ministry. One thing I've noticed is that you can expect to hear the same songs over and over again. Mercy Me's *I Can Only Imagine* is a funeral standard. Occasionally I still encounter Ray Boltz's song *Thank You for Giving to the Lord*. The truth is, there are less and less songs being written about heaven and eternity these days, and as a result, our theology of heaven is shallow, and our conviction about eternity is weak.

I ask you worship leader: if it was solely based on the songs you lead, what would a dying saint know about their life after death? Most of us can do a better job in this area of our leadership. If our songs will shepherd the dying into eternity, let's begin now to do the work of providing for them a theological foundation of death and heaven that will give them and their grieving families comfort when that season of life approaches.

WORSHIP PASTORING THE GRIEVING FAMILY

There is a significant element involved with the worship pastor comforting a dying saint about to meet God and that is his role in ministering to the family that is grieving and hurting. Songs are incredibly effective at ministering in this way. Like a dying patent singing songs of praise, the family can also be comforted by this expression of worship as well.

As part of my doctoral thesis, I conducted a survey with over one hundred people in which one of the questions asked was if they had ever sung hymns or worship songs around a dying loved one. The survey showed more than half (51.38%) of people said they had.[48]

This tells me, like before, the worship pastor must be intentional in his worship planning and have moments like this in mind. Whether or not the worship minister is by the hospital bed leading in the singing, his influence will be made known during moments like this.

Another aspect of comforting the grieving family is during the funeral planning process. While the relatives are making funeral arrangements and organizing the logistics of laying to rest their loved one, this is an incredible opportunity to pastor them. This is a time the worship leader can be more to them than simply a musician-for-hire. The presence of the worship pastor during this process will mean a great deal to the loved ones. This will be a time to be able to encourage them, serve them, cry with them, and pray with them.

The songs the worship pastor sings at the funeral will not only honor the dead, but will stay with the family forever. Another aspect of my thesis survey revealed that 66% of the people surveyed stated there was a hymn or worship song connected to the memory of a deceased loved one.[49] This proves the worship pastor has significant impact in the lives of people that lasts far beyond the experience of a worship gathering.

Long after the sermon is given, the obituary is read, and the funeral guests all go home and get back to their routines of life,

---

48   Zeb Balentine, *Doxology and Discipleship*, 74.
49   Ibid. 74.

the songs are sung at their loved one's funerals will have a special impact throughout the life of the family of the deceased. The songs will help prepare them for their own appointed day when they step into eternity.

I also asked the subjects of my survey to name the song. Hymns outnumbered modern songs three to one. This tells me that either old hymn writers did a better job as spiritual "morticians" and "care-takers" than songwriters of today. This reveals a significant need for worship planners and songwriters to make an intentional effort to minister to the Body of Christ with seasons like this in mind.

By singing like care-takers, we are helping to shape a theology of death, grieving, life, eternal life, God's sovereignty, and Christ ultimately defeating death when He rose from the grave. Death comes to all. We must do our part as singing pastors and spiritual caretakers to help prepare people and shape their hearts and minds for the final season of this life.

CHAPTER 8

SING LIKE FAMILY MEN

"I am a family man. I traded in my mustang for a minivan."
–Andrew Peterson, *"Family Man"*

Picture yourself as a husband and a dad who works as a worship leader at a local church. You are good at your job and receive tons of affirmation from your congregation, your pastor, and even those in the community that are not part of your church. God has gifted you with skills, talents, and spiritual gifts. Mix that with a strong work ethic and you have a successful music ministry.

Day in and day out, you work hard planning and preparing for awesome worship gatherings. Maybe you spent all night the night before rehearsing. Or you just had a Sunday morning worship service and nailed it. After the service, you are flooded with compliments of how talented you are, how hard you work, or what a great worship experience that was. You gave it your all, and it paid off.

You come home completely exhausted because you have given all of yourself, and if not all, easily the best part to the church. There isn't much of you left to give, so you decide to veg out in front of the television. Eventually, this isn't just Sundays or rehearsal days, but becomes a nightly pattern. Your wife and kids begin to notice on evenings in which you are actually home, you aren't really home. You might be in front of the television, tinkering in the garage, or playing on the smartphone. Or you even bring work home with you.

Perhaps you aren't the kind of dad and husband that checks out when you get home. Maybe you are good at making sure your family has your attention. Perhaps you spend quality time with them, but not so much on a spiritual level.

Imagine the same worship leader dad, except he is the kind that comes home and everyone lights up for him because they know they will have his attention. The kids know it's play time. He spends a few moments wrestling with the son. After that, he goes into his daughter's room for a make-believe tea party. Next, he goes into the kitchen to chat with his wife and talk about how each of their days went while he helps cook dinner. After dinner, he volunteers to clean up. After the dishes are done, he helps bathe the kids, get them dressed for bed and makes sure they brush their teeth. He kisses them goodnight and everyone goes to sleep, with no mention of Christ, Scripture, or prayer.

This guy is far from being an absent father and husband. In fact, he is faithfully involved in the lives of his wife and kids. But when he checks out of being a career worship leader, he never checks in to being the family worship leader.

There could be seasons in your life in which you might find yourself being like one of these dads. Both of these examples are falling short of what we, as Christian, worship-leading, family-men are called to be. Both examples represent men who thrive at work. They are dynamic worship leaders in the public and on the platform, but at home when they are away from the stage, the lights, and the audience, they are absolutely dropping the ball.

We've all been there. I've found myself, at different times, looking like both of these examples. But, if we are going to be faithful worship leaders and faithful singing teachers, our first responsibility is to faithfully and consistently lead our families by teaching them about Who God is and what He has done. Your family members are part of the church you are called to serve, and I would argue, they are the most important members of your church. If your ministry to the rest of the church fails, you will still have your family. But, if your ministry to your family fails, even when your church ministry is thriving, you will lose your influence within the entire church. Bottom line, if we strive to lead the church with excellence, but we fail to lead our families well, we are hypocrites. If we want to influence and teach the church sound doctrine, it begins in the home. Our families are the first church members we are called and entrusted to teach, train, and disciple.

ASAPH'S EXAMPLE

When it comes to men who have proven themselves to be faithful in balancing their worship-leading responsibilities with their family-leading responsibilities, I can't think of any better than Asaph. He was a Levitical singer (2 Chronicles 5:12). He was responsible for helping lead the musical worship when the Israelites gathered.

His sons also followed in his footsteps (1 Chronicles 25:1) as was God's plan for the Levites (Exodus 32:29). He was faithful to lead God's children in worship, but more importantly, he was faithful to lead HIS OWN children as well. He left a legacy with his family and they were faithful people who knew, loved, and obeyed their Lord.

Asaph wrote several of the Psalms, One in particular was Psalm seventy-eight and it's known as the "Trans-Generational Commission." This Psalm so named because of the charge for the worshiper to evangelize their children and future generations. It describes the purpose of these children growing up to become faithful worshipers of God who seek to know Him and to make Him known. Let's take a look at what Asaph, the worship leader, had to say about being a disciple-making family-man. Also notice these truths and admonishments are in a song:

Verses two and three state:

I will open my mouth in a parable;
I will utter dark sayings from of old,
things that we have heard and known,
that our fathers have told us.

Asaph declares he has a message to give. He's not communicating it with his lifestyle, which is still important, but he's actually opening his mouth and proclaiming the message verbally. This is an old message passed down to him from his fathers. Now, think about that. What do we do with valuable and precious things? They become family heirlooms. We are intentional with being good stewards of them and we make sure we pass them down to our children. It is made clear to them they are to do the same.

My great-grandfather was a musician. He used to play the fiddle in a country band. He was actually brought under church discipline for playing his fiddle in bars. I now own his old fiddle. I have no idea how much money it's worth. It's probably in the thousands. It is an incredibly valuable thing that has been passed down from generations. This instrument is not something I will sell to a pawn shop for a few bucks to spend on gas or pizza. It's not something that will be left and forgotten somewhere. I know exactly where it is at this very moment. I take good care of it, and I have full intention of passing it down to one of my children.

The same should be said about the gospel. The most precious family heirloom we can pass down to our children is a legacy of knowing, loving, and following Christ. Asaph's dad was faithful to pass this down to him, and Asaph made sure he passed it down to his children. Worship leader, will you be faithful to pass down this message of God to your family?

He continues in verse four:

We will not hide them from their children,
but tell the coming generation the glorious deeds of the
LORD,
and his might, and the wonders that he has done.

Notice what he says here. He says that he will not "hide" these things from their children. To neglect teaching our families about who God is and what He has done is to hide those things from them. Why would we hide such good, life-giving, soul-saving truths from those we love the most? Our most valuable possession hidden from our most valuable people?

> *He established a testimony in Jacob and appointed a law in Israel,*
> *which he commanded our fathers to teach to their children,*
> *that the next generation might know them, the children yet unborn,*
> *and arise and tell them to their children... (verses 5-6)*

He notes God's command and plan for His message to continue to pass down from generation to generation. Why is this? Why is it such a big deal? Check out verse seven:

> *...so that they should set their hope in God and not forget the works of God,*
> *but keep his commandments;*

The reason? So our children will have a saving hope and will not forget the works of God. The souls of our children are what's at stake. And not just our children, but the souls of our grand-children's grand-children. The world around us is quickly growing more hostile to God. More than ever, people view the church, the Bible, and Jesus as irrelevant to their lives, and professing Christians are living as such. Do you want your family to be the one that forgets the Lord? Then remind them. Frequently. We work hard at excelling in our jobs as worship leaders and singing teachers publicly, our real ministry happens in our living rooms, at our dinner tables, and beside the beds of our children. We are in a fight for their souls. Let's strive to be intentional and faithful to teach our families about the Person and Work of God so they will have their hope in Him.

Verse eight says something interesting, sobering, and seemingly contradictory:

> *...and that they should not be like their fathers, a stubborn and rebellious generation,*
> *a generation whose heart was not steadfast, whose spirit was not faithful to God.*

Notice the characteristics of Asaph's forefathers that he describes here. He says future generations shouldn't be like them. They are stubborn, rebellious, their hearts were not steadfast, and their spirits were not faithful to God. Wow, that's some pretty heavy accusations. But it's strange that even with all of those negative terms used to describe them, according to verse three, they still taught their children about God. If the Scripture says all of these sobering things about that generation's spiritual slothfulness, but they still taught their children the things of God, what would it say about us if we neglect to do even that?

WHY DO WE FALL SHORT?

There are those few guys that seem to lead in family worship and discipleship so perfectly. They never miss a day and when they have worship time, their children sit still like perfect angels, never getting distracted and always participating, and it seems like any moment the heavens will open and Jesus Himself will reach His hand down and give the dad a high-five and a big thumbs up.

For the rest of us, especially those of us with small children, family worship time can look more like the movie "Gremlins." Children are climbing on the furniture, hanging from the ceiling fan, and lighting stuff on fire. At times, family worship can look less like a worship service and more like an exorcism. That's okay. It's supposed to be messy. That's normal. The important thing is that we are faithful to lead our families.

Having unrealistic expectations can often discourage us from being the worship leaders at home that we are on the platform. It requires intentionality, consistency, and great patience. Remember, the enemy doesn't want us to do this. He will try to discourage and frustrate us. Don't let him win. Remember, God has commanded this of us, so He is on our side. He's with us and for us.

But, why do we forget this? Why do we tend to fail in this area of our life and ministry? This is simply an echo of the Fall. In Genesis chapter three, we see that Adam neglected his responsibility as a spiritual leader. God gave Adam the command not to eat of the tree of the knowledge of good and evil (2:17), and he was trusted to communicate that to Eve. He did a poor job of that as Eve didn't really understand the command. She adds to it, "...neither shall you touch it..." (3:3), she doubted it (6a), and she eventually disobeyed it (6b). Now men tend to jokingly blame Eve for this, but the New Testament holds Adam fully responsible (Romans 6). After all, it was he who failed to communicate God's truth to her, and instead of protecting her from the lures of the Serpent, he stood there like a schmuck and let it happen.

Because we are all fallen sons of Adam, we have the tendency to neglect our responsibilities as family-men. Our proclivity is to stand around like spiritually passive fools and give Satan an all-access pass to destroy our families. We are naturally bent to be spiritually neglectful of our responsibilities in our homes. But we must fight against that. We must be determined to do better.

WHAT DO WE DO?

Family worship and discipleship looks different for each family. Typically, at my house, we have three staple elements of our worship times together: singing, scripture, and prayer. Everything we do usually falls under those three elements. Here are some practical suggestions I've gleaned from others more experienced and wiser than I am.

HYMN OF THE MONTH

I once heard Keith and Kristyn Getty speaking on family worship and discipleship and among other things, they always have a "hymn of the month" at their house. Following the spirit of Colossians 3:16 and knowing how effective singing is at shaping our theology and how many hymns are theologically rich, the Gettys spend an entire month singing and learning a hymn together as a family. I have adopted this in my home as well and have found it to be very effective. We learn about one verse of the hymn a week and by the end of the month, we have learned the whole thing. We stop and talk about what certain words or lines mean, and we choose a Scripture verse to memorize that goes with the theme of the hymn, and our children are learning a ton of theology by doing this.

DELEGATE

As children get older, I think it's important to give them ownership in this experience and allow them to have a role in family worship. From the beginning, each of my children have a time where they pray. Everyone else remains silent, with their heads bowed and eyes closed as each person of our family takes a moment to pray. My oldest son is now getting to the age where he will occasionally tell a Bible story or read a Scripture verse. My vision for our family worship is that one day, each member of my family will take turns choosing the hymn of the month, teaching it to the family, discussing why they chose the hymn and what it teaches us about God. I would also like to have each of my children select Scripture or bring a Bible thought to our time together. Maybe your children are at an age where you can delegate tasks to them. This will be effective and they will remember it forever.

DISCUSS

I encourage you as you are leaving church on Sunday morning, whether you are rushing to get to a restaurant or home to get a hot meal, take time to slow down and talk with your family about the songs you just sang together. Chances are they may not always pay attention to or remember the details of the sermon (hopefully they will, but realistically they won't every single time), but they will likely remember the songs that were sung.

Ask them which one was their favorite and why. Talk about specific lyrics. Talk about what the song made them think or how it made them feel. This is not a structured time of family discipleship, but it is intentional, and it is an example of how we can teach them when we "walk by the way." (Deuteronomy 6:7)

SURROUND YOURSELF WITH SINGING

I would encourage you to surround yourself and your family with worship music. This doesn't have to be stuff heard on Christian radio. I am also not making a case that the only thing you listen to should be worship music. My family and I are music lovers and even my small children already have good taste. My sweet, shy, daughter asks me frequently to play "Sweet Child O' Mine" by Guns N' Roses...and I always comply. I digress.

While I am happy about the fact that my children love music and that they love GOOD stuff, I also try to be very intentional with it, and use it as something that is not solely for entertainment, but also for edification. Whether we are driving in the car or eating at the dinner table, we try to have songs playing. Often times, the tunes we play for our children is doctrinally rich worship songs. Try making a playlist of songs you want your family to be listening to, learning, and singing along with. This will be especially helpful to those families who are not musically gifted. Make technology work for you.

Make no mistake about it, the influence we have as worship pastors over the Body of Christ doesn't end when the singing stops on Sunday morning. Our songs shape the hearts and minds of those who sing them. And our influence in the church continues when we are at home in our living rooms, around the dinner table, or kneeling down beside the beds of our children as we sing and pray to our Lord.

BIBLIOGRAPHY

- Balentine, Zeb. Doxology and Discipleship: Principles for How the Worship Leader Functions Pastorally, Lynchburg, VA: Liberty University, 2017.

- Best, Harold M. Music Through the Eyes of Faith, New York, NY: Harper One Publishers, 1973.

- Best, Harold M. Unceasing Worship: Biblical Perspectives on Worship and the Arts, Downers Grove, IL: InterVarsity Press, 2003.

- Charles, H. B. On Pastoring: A Short Guide to Living, Leading, and Ministering as a Pastor, Chicago, IL: Moody Publishers, 2016.

- Cherry, Constance. The Worship Architect: A Blueprint for Designing Culturally Relevant and Biblically Faithful Services, Grand Rapids, MI: Baker Academic, 2010.

- Corbitt, J. Nathan. The Sound of the Harvest: Music's Mission in Church and Culture, Grand Rapids, MI; Baker Books, 1998.

- Dever, Mark and Paul Alexander. The Deliberate Church: Building Your Ministry on the Gospel, Wheaton, IL: Crossway, 2005.

- Hicks, Zac. The Worship Pastor: A Call to Ministry for Worship Leaders and Teams, Grand Rapids, MI: Zondervan, 2016.

- Jancke, Lutz. "Music, Memory and Emotion." 7, no. 21 (Published online Aug 8, 2008): Accessed Feb 28, 2017. https://www.ncbi.nlm.nih.gov/pmc/articles/PMC2776393/

- Kauflin, Bob. Why Do We Sing?—Colossians 3:16-17, Sovereign Grace Church, November 25, 2012. Accessed March 28, 2017.

- Kauflin, Bob. Worship Matters: Leading Others to Encounter with Greatness of God, Wheaton, IL: Crossway, 2008.

- Kraeuter, Tom. Keys to Becoming an Effective Worship Leader, Lynwood, WA: Emerald Books, 2011.

- Miller, Stephen. Worship Leaders, We Are Not Rock Stars, Chicago, IL: Moody Publishers, 2013.

- Morgenthaler, Sally. Worship Evangelism: Inviting Unbelievers into the Presence of God, Grand Rapids, MI: Zondervan, 1995.

- Page, Frank S. and L. Lavon Gray. Hungry for Worship: Challenges and Solutions for Today's Church, Birmingham, AL: New Hope Publishers, 2014.

- Piper, John. Let the Nations Be Glad! The Supremacy of God in Missions, Grand Rapids, MI: Baker Academic. 1993.

- Raglio, Alfredo. (2012). "Music Therapy in Dementia." Dementia: Non-Pharmacological Therapies (pp. 1-14). Nova Science Publishers, Inc. Accessed on February 28, 2017.

- Sacks, Oliver W. Musicophilia: Takes of Music and the Brain, New York, NY: Knopf, 2007.

- Sacks, Oliver. "The Power of Music." Brain Volume 129, issue 10 (October 1, 2006): Accessed on February 28, 2017. https://doi.org/10.1093/brain/awl234

- Segler, Franklin M. and Randall Bradley, Christian Worship: Its Theology and Practice, Nashville, TN: B&H Publishing, 2006.

- Stott, John. The Contemporary Christian: Applying God's Word to Today's World, Downers Grove, IL: InterVarsity Press, 1995.

- Towns, Elmer L. and Vernon M. Whaley. Worship Through the Ages: How the Great Awakenings Shape Evangelical Worship, Nashville, TN: B&H Academic, 2012.

- Walters, Michael. Can't Wait for Sunday: Leading Your Congregation in Authentic Worship, Indianapolis, IN: Wesleyan Publishing House, 2006.

- Wiersbe, Warren. Real Worship: Playground, Battle Ground, or Holy Ground?, Grand Rapids, MI: Baker Books, 2000.

- Witvliet, John D. Worship Seeking Understanding: Windows into Christian Practice, Grand Rapids, MI: Baker Books, 2003.

You have a story.
We want to publish it.

Everyone has as a story to tell. It might be about something you know how to do, or what has happened in your life, or it may be a thrilling, or romantic, or intriguing, or heartwarming, or suspenseful story, starring a cast of characters that have been swimming around in your imagination.

And at Wyatt House Publishing, we can get your story onto the pages of a book just like the one you are holding in your hand. With professional interior design and a custom, professionally designed cover built just for you from the start, you can finally see your dream of being an author become reality. Then, you will see your book listed with retailers all over the world as people are able to buy your book from wherever they are and have it delivered to their home or their e-reader.

So what are you waiting for? This is your time.

visit us at
www.wyattpublishing.com

for details on how to get started becoming a
published author right away.

CPSIA information can be obtained
at www.ICGtesting.com
Printed in the USA
LVHW041002040319
609387LV00004B/490